SADDLERY

SADDLERY

Modern Equipment for Horse and Stable

E. HARTLEY EDWARDS

Foreword by Lieut.-Colonel Frank Weldon

A. S. Barnes and Company, Inc.

Printed in the United States of America

ACKNOWLEDGMENTS

My acknowledgments and grateful thanks are due to:

Lieut.-Colonel Frank Weldon, M.V.O., M.B.E., M.C., for his kindness in consenting to write a foreword to this book.

Lieut.-Colonel F. E. Gibson, M.B.E., who gave me the opportunity to enter the saddlery trade and whose guidance in all aspects of saddlery has been the basis of all the knowledge which I have acquired.

Mrs G. C. Morrison, for typing, collating and correcting my manuscript.

Miss M. Robinette, for line illustrations.

Messrs Turf and Travel Ltd, for the loan of blocks.

E. H. E.

CONTENTS

FOREWORD

By Lieut.-Colonel F. W. C. Weldon, M.V.O., M.B.E., M.C.

It is remarkable how ignorant most of us are about the saddlery and equipment we use every day, which is just as indispensable as the horse himself to our favourite recreation or sport—how it is made, what it is made of and how to get the best out of it.

I have been using it as much as anyone for forty years, yet from this book I have learned much that I did not know, and some of the bits and appliances, whose function and use are explained, were little more than romantic names before. It is not that I despise 'gadgets' on principle, be they martingales, nosebands, the more severe bits or other contrivances. I take the view that if we ride for pleasure, it is plain stupid not to employ any device which undeniably improves our safety, confidence or ease of control in times of stress. However, it would be wise to heed the author's warning in his introduction to 'The Principles and Mechanics of Bitting' before clutching gratefully at some ingenious device which in less skilled hands may only produce a worse problem in the end. There is no short cut to success at anything to do with riding, no lasting good ever came out of the use of force, and there is no substitute for sympathy, patience or tact; so the simplest, most direct means of communication will probably be best in the long run.

Undoubtedly the greatest contribution to the art of equitation in the last twenty years has been made by the saddlers who have developed the modern, spring-tree saddle. Not only does it put the rider willy-nilly into the most convenient position for the horse to bear his weight and understand his signals, but it is infinitely more comfortable to sit in and, above all, almost impossible to fall out of. I would no more dream of using a conventional hunting saddle in preference to a modern General Purpose one for hacking, hunting, jumping or cross-country riding than I would pick a kitchen stool rather than a well-upholstered armchair for a Sunday afternoon nap.

9

If this book only serves to encourage some of its readers to ride better and get more pleasure out of riding, then in this respect alone it will have succeeded admirably; but it will do much more. Never before has anyone attempted to explain in simple language the use and purpose of the bewildering variety of equipment and clothing which has been devised for the comfort and protection of the horse both in the stable and at work. Pray Heaven that we shall never have to buy all of it at once, but how convenient to have such a reference book handy and to be able to look up the best solution to the crisis of the moment.

INTRODUCTION

Saddlery and its application in the widest sense, I have found to be somewhat of an unknown quantity as far as the great majority of the riding public is concerned; this is no doubt due to the fact that there is very little written information about it. I have, therefore, attempted in this book to give as comprehensive an account as possible of the range, scope and variety of articles available within this particular field.

It is by no means the authoritative work of reference I had originally planned some years ago and for which I have, unfortunately, not had time; it is based on a series of lecture notes, which I hope will nevertheless help to bridge the gap.

1963   E. H. E.

1 LEATHER

'There is nothing . . . like leather'

Before we think of saddlery as bridles, girths and so on, let us consider the first basic material of the saddlery trade, which is leather. Just we we should know something of the construction and functions of the horse's body, if we are to keep him in good health, so we should know something about the materials used in the making of our tack if it is to be kept in similar condition and give us the service we require.

The cow—or, more correctly, the bovine species—is the source of ninety per cent of the leather used in saddlery; the best coming from young stock, with the hide of the Aberdeen Angus being considered exceptionally good.

However, the production of British hides can in no way satisfy the enormous demand for leather goods of all kinds and the greater proportion of hides is, therefore, imported from the Argentine and the Continent, the advantage of these over our British ones being the absence from them of barbed-wire and warble marks. Such marks, while not weakening the hide, disfigure it and make for uneconomical cutting. The hides are imported in their rough state, the currying process being carried out in this country where the art of leather dressing is possibly the most highly developed in the world.

Part of the remaining ten per cent is obtained from the skins of pig and sheep, the latter being reserved for the backing of saddle panels and linings of cheaper saddles, etc. Saddlery pigskin has little *substance* (this is a word to remember and refers to the actual thickness of the leather) and this property, combining with that of elasticity, makes it ideal for the making of the saddle seat. The skin is put on the prepared saddle tree in a damp condition, enabling it to be stretched tightly so that on drying a neat, tight seat is produced. There are, of course, other small jobs for which pigskin is used in a saddlery shop, but the making of the saddle seat is its main one. When giving lectures it is at this point that

I perceive surreptitious nudgings and whisperings among my audience. At one time I found this disconcerting, but now I forestall the inevitable question and say firmly: 'If you think you have a *pigskin* saddle—you haven't!'

The flaps and skirts of the saddle—that is, the whole top with the exception of the seat itself—are made from cowhide embossed with a grain to match the characteristic bristle marks of the pigskin. Because of its light substance, pigskin would be quite unsuitable for the flaps and skirts, which for practical purposes must be of heavier quality. The only occasion when a saddle is made entirely of pigskin is in the case of the very light racing saddles weighing, unmounted, anything from 8 oz. to $2\frac{1}{2}$ lb. (the weight of a hunting saddle being anything from 11 to 14 lb.).

The reason for the widespread belief that a saddle is made from pigskin probably arises from the pre-war practice of covering the cowhide skirts and flaps with pigskin—in other words a pigskin-*covered* saddle. In many cases this produced a saddle of unimpeachable craftsmanship combined with a remarkable and board-like rigidity of the flaps. It is possible that by the third generation of riders and the application of much grease, the flap might have softened sufficiently to be of practical use, but it must have given the original owner considerable discomfort.

Similarly a 'doeskin' saddle is in reality a saddle on which the flaps and skirts of cowhide are covered in doeskin, although in this case the seat would be from doeskin and not from pig. Doeskin-covered saddles are, of course, fairly common and even today the occasional pigskin-covered saddle is made. When this is done it is necessary to employ a cowhide of much lighter substance if one is to maintain the desirable suppleness in the flap.

Having digressed somewhat let us now consider briefly the hands through which the leather passes before it is bought by the saddler. Initially the hide is removed from the carcase and passes to the tanner who, briefly again, with the use of chemicals and greases, renders what was a perishable article into an imperishable one.

The currier, on whom falls a great deal of responsibility, then takes over the hide to dress and finish it, and this is achieved by a series of processes during which oils and greases are incorporated into the leather to give increased tensile strength, flexibility and water-resisting properties.

It is important that the hide should have plenty of *substance* (i.e.

thickness), for it follows that the greater this is, the greater will be the fat-content of that particular hide with a corresponding improvement in the flexibility and wearing properties.

One must also remember that leather, to make perhaps an obvious assertion, has two sides, a *flesh* side and a *grain* side. The latter refers to the outside, which during the course of the final dressing becomes sealed and nearly waterproof and, at the same time, has its *colour* finally determined. While most saddles and bridles are a yellow colour, known as London colour, it is not necessary for this to be so if the saddler stipulates a variation of this basic colour. Apart from London colour, bridle or saddle leather can be either 'Havana', the colour of a good cigar, or 'Warwick', a much darker colour. Obviously these colours will vary from one currier to another and may even alter slightly in the hands of an individual currier. London, when a yellow orange shade, is a pleasant colour, and soon tones down well. It is probably the most common and is always in demand for the export market; but if you dislike your tack to look new, then you can buy saddlery made in one of the other colours. Havana, for instance, is a good colour which grows old gracefully; the darker Warwick is perhaps not so satisfactory as it frequently becomes black and flat-looking after a time.

The quality and wearing value of leather is in no way affected by its colour, although it is unlikely that you will buy a cheap article in a good Havana shade.

Having mentioned the question of price, let me say that saddlery made from the very best leather can never be cheap. The tanning and the currying process is a hand one, just as is the making of saddlery, and such leather may well stay with the currier for many weeks, thereby increasing its value. Obviously a bad hide of poor and irregular substance is not worth a great deal of time and attention, and while it will cost less its quality will be poor and saddlery made from it will be expensive in the long run for the wrong reasons. Many curriers and saddlers, too, like to keep their finished hides in store for some weeks before using them, so that they have a chance to mature and, while the customer will benefit from such a practice, money thus tied up means an increase in cost.

A saddler does not necessarily buy a whole hide as such, but in the various portions which are applicable to the articles he wishes to produce.

From the diagram (Fig. 1) you will see that the hide has been divided into sections. The best part of the hide is on either side of the backbone, and for bridle leather a butt is asked for and in some cases a full back—that is, the full length from tail to neck when a particular length is required. A saddle flap is also made from a butt having an embossed finish to match the pigskin of the seat. The shoulder of the hide is stout, cheaper to buy, but coarser

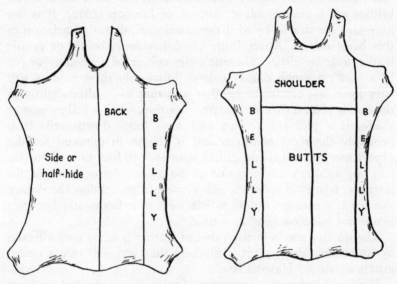

1. Sections of hide.

in texture and is used for head collar work and in cheap saddles for flap leather. It is not suitable for pure bridle work. As one gets lower down the flanks the quality, texture and substance deteriorates and the actual belly is useful only for odd jobs, being otherwise too thin for work requiring a substantial leather. It is interesting to note that from one hide the saddler can make just four first-class bridles from that part of the butt on either side of the backbone.

While most horse people (by divine right?) consider themselves competent to criticise the quality of leather, or at least to qualify their criticisms by saying 'Well, I'm not an expert, of course, but I do know a good piece of leather when I see one', I will (as a saddler and not a currier), for the benefit of those in whom the precept of divine right may be not so firmly entrenched, give a few pointers as to what I think they should look for in a piece of leather.

First, as I have said, good leather has plenty of *substance* or thickness. The greater this is, the greater is the possible fat content which is its life blood.

Secondly, the *flesh* side (the inside) should be smooth in texture and there should be no rough, loose fibres visible.

Thirdly, the leather should feel slightly greasy and should in no way be dry.

Fourthly, it should be firm and not soft or pappy to the touch.

Lastly, when the leather is bent in the hand, neither side should form bubbles on the skin.

A last word on *substance*; this will vary according to the requirements of the finished article, a body roller, for instance, requiring a greater degree of this than a bridle. A show bridle, where the object is to produce an elegant article, will be made from leather of a lighter substance than a hunting bridle which will be expected to stand up to harder usage. A moral here—if you want a show bridle and intend to use it for hunting as well, let the saddler know and effect a compromise. If you ask for the lightest possible bridle, and then use it as an everyday one, do not be surprised if the saddler is not entirely sympathetic when you complain that it has not worn very well.

Many people today like to have their saddle flaps made in a very light substance, so that there is little resistance to the leg positioning, and the quality of leather dressed to meet this requirement remains unaffected, but obviously it will not wear for as long as flaps of a heavier type. For my part, I would prefer to have light supple flaps (providing they were not so light as to roll under my leg) and to renew them every few years rather than to have the longer lasting but uncomfortably rigid flap of the stronger variety.

You will probably have met various words describing certain leathers which may need clarification. One of the common ones that comes to mind is split *rawhide*, which is again a cowhide subjected to a special vegetable tannage. It can be easily recognised, as this treatment leaves an untanned central layer which appears as a line of lighter colour running through the centre of the leather when viewed edgewise. It is immensely strong and hard and is used for stirrup leathers, girth straps, etc.

Helvetia leather, often confused with rawhide, is on the other hand exceptionally greasy and tough. It is yellow in colour and used for reinforcing nosebands, martingales and the like and occasionally for making certain types of dropped or show-jumping nosebands.

You will also see, principally on stirrup leathers, the words 'Oak bark tanned'. These will be cowhide leathers of the best quality and the description applies to the special and very lengthy treatment the leather has undergone.

The red-coloured stirrup leathers, which are deservedly popular, are often termed incorrectly rawhide. They are in fact made from buffalo hides and are invariably slightly greasy, very soft and virtually unbreakable.

Doeskin or buckskin is extremely expensive and is, as its name implies, not related to cowhide, but is a suède leather made from deerskin, and used for the covering of saddles. There are, however, mock doeskins (mutton dressed not in this case as lamb but deer!) which are cheaper, but these should always be described as 'mock doeskins'.

Neither doe nor mock doe should be confused with reversed hide. Saddles are very frequently made in this leather, which is simply a cowhide with the grain side scuffed up by machine to give a rough hairy surface. Such a surface affords considerable grip in the early days of its life and is often helpful for either small children or for those of us who require every possible assistance to stay in the plate. In time the rough surface will wear smooth, but this final stage can be delayed by repeated applications of a wire brush or even a little sandpaper. Reversed hide is no more expensive than an ordinary finish.

THE CARE AND CLEANING OF LEATHER

I have previously referred to leather as (*a*) having two sides, a *flesh* side and a *grain* side and (*b*) as having a fat content which is its life blood. If we appreciate these two points we are half-way to looking after our tack so that it will give us the best possible service.

Let us deal first with the fat content. Leather loses a percentage of this constituent every day of its life, and just as we need food to replace our used energy so leather needs constant replenishment of its particular 'life blood' if it is to continue to lead a useful life. In its fight for survival *water*, *heat* and *neglect* are the three main enemies with which leather has to contend and which deprive it of this vital commodity. Water, particularly if it is hot, melts and removes the fat, whereas heat dries it out. Every time a bridle or a girth is used, for example, it loses some of its fat content on account of heat from the horse and sweat from his body, and this results in the leather becoming dry and brittle. It is not necessary, therefore, to throw a bridle into a bucket of hot water after hunting—a damp sponge is far the best thing to use. It is equally stupid to hang a wet bridle over the kitchen range or to drape it over a radiator; in both cases, for reasons which I have described, the leather will become dry, brittle and dangerous.

There are, however, a number of preparations on the market, that will keep leather supple; *Kocholine*, a red jelly-like substance is one, *Flexalan* is another. But before applying them it is essential to remember the differences between the two sides of leather—the flesh and the grain. The grain side has been waterproofed and the pores have been sealed, whereas the flesh side has not received this sealing to any extent and the pores are therefore open and ready to receive and to lose the nourishment that leather requires.

If then we appreciate this point and, when cleaning tack, first make sure of removing the sweat deposits which will have formed on the flesh side, thus blocking the pores, we will accordingly apply the nourishment more to this side than to the grain side. Then when the bridle is clean and dry, the preparation of our choice can be rubbed in with the fingers on the flesh side and the bridle subsequently finished off with saddle soap, preferably of the glycerine variety applied with a *slightly* damp (not wet) sponge. Polished with a chamois leather, the bridle should acquire a sheen combined with a good supple feel.

Saddles should be treated with saddle soap on the outside and with *Kocholine*, or something similar, on the flesh or under side of the flaps so that the grease will work through and keep them soft. Too much grease applied to the outside of your saddle will not be absorbed, and a pair of very stained breeches will be an indication of your misplaced zeal!

Saddle soap should be used regularly every day and a dressing of grease given perhaps once weekly. Needless to say, you cannot clean a bridle properly without taking it to pieces first. Any saddlery being stored for a long period should be treated generously with *Kocholine* and buckles, etc., should be smeared with it to prevent corrosion.

The chief cause, as we have seen, of the deterioration in leather is loss of fat content as a result of neglect, but it is possible to go too far in the other direction and overfeed the leather. Used in this way the preparations which I have mentioned will just make the tack unpleasantly greasy, but should you be a devotee of neatsfoot oil, the result will be even more serious. If this is used to excess (and many people with new tack soak it in neatsfoot oil to darken it) the leather, being unable to absorb the surfeit of nourishment, will lose its tenacity, becoming flabby and greasy and in fact oozing oil at every opportunity. Just as the human body loses its efficiency if it over-indulges itself in high living, so leather will suffer in the way I have indicated for somewhat similar reasons.

Occasionally show head collars and the like are polished with boot polish, but I would not recommend this treatment for articles in everyday use, because boot polish tends to seal the pores of leather which will crack in time. If it is used on a saddle one slides from front to rear quite beautifully!

The chances of well-looked-after, supple leather breaking in normal use are not very great, but neglected leather will give one day and the fault will be its owner's. Leather, or bridle leather anyway, is not unbreakable and if you allow your horse to tread on his rein or if you tie him up with a rein and he runs back, it is more than likely it will snap. The point I wish to make is that under those circumstances do not blame either the leather ('It must have been poor quality leather') or the saddler, but indeed yourself.

2 METALS

'All that glistens is not gold'

The second basic material connected with the production of saddlery is metal. In our grandfather's day bits and irons were made from steel, either hand-forged or drop-forged, and produced in far greater variety than is possible today. These bits were of exceptional strength, beautifully made and finished. They were not, however, rustless, but with cheap and plentiful labour this hardly mattered. To clean them a burnisher and a little sand were employed and the curb chains duly swung in a stable rubber.

Today all bits and irons are rustless, but few can compare with the workmanship displayed in these old bits. There are still many about, and if you have one or two in the corner of the tack room they can be cleaned and chrome-plated. The chrome-plating will wear off in time, and if you live near the sea the salt air will remove it even more quickly, but the plating can, of course, be renewed and the operation is not an expensive one.

Of the metals available today, all of which are enormously important and an essential factor in our safety, there are three or four main types used in the manufacture of buckles, fittings, bits, irons, spurs, etc., not including brass, which is confined to buckles alone.

First of these is solid nickel, which is rustless and cheap; it has no other virtue. It turns yellow quickly, it will bend and it will break. A sharp knock on a gate-post is enough to break an iron, or even a sudden application of weight is enough to cause a fracture, and a strong-pulling horse can easily bend the ring of a nickel bit. I would neither use it nor recommend it. For children it might be permissible, but I would rather they had stirrup irons made of malleable iron, plated, than made of solid nickel. In short, I have yet to work out why nickel should be graced with the bastion-like prefix of 'solid'!

There are then what I term the Named Nickel Mixtures, which are in a different category entirely; on bits and irons of this metal you will find a trade name stamped. The best known is perhaps Eglantine and others are Kangaroo and Premier, but all are good and reliable. They maintain their colour, are rustless, and breakages are few and far between. At one time Eglantine bits in particular were available in a wide range of patterns and were really well finished; today the metal is as dependable, but the finish, owing to the lack of skilled finishers, may not be near the pre-war standard. The price in this category is more than twice that of solid nickel, but well worth it.

Probably the most popular metal today is stainless steel. It is rustless, with a good bright appearance and, while not unbreakable, is very nearly so. The range of bit patterns is a little restricted (for which the horse at least may be grateful), and the finish is perhaps not as good as Eglantine, but it is certainly reliable and deserves its good name.

All articles made from these metals are cast in a mould and are then finished and polished by machine and hand. The variety of type and size of bits and stirrup irons available is, therefore, dependent on the number of pattern moulds held by the manufacturer; and as patterns are expensive, it is not possible to have an article made up in these metals to some peculiar shape or size outside the scope of existing patterns, unless you are prepared to stand the cost of a gross or two, or can persuade your saddler to do so.

Up to a few years ago it was possible to obtain the aristocrat of all metals—hand-forged, stainless steel. Bits and irons, made and finished throughout by hand, were works of art and you could order any size or shape you required. The price was high, but the article was of the finest quality and would last indefinitely. If one is patient, it is still possible to obtain an odd bit or a pair of irons, but it is unlikely that we shall ever see articles of hand-forged stainless steel on the market again in any quantity.

Lastly, there is aluminium, from which a number of racing bits and irons are manufactured. For this purpose they have the advantage of extreme lightness in weight and, while they may be safe enough for racing on the flat, I would otherwise view this metal with extreme caution—particularly as a recent Grand National may well have been lost through the breaking of an aluminium iron.

No metal is, or can be, guaranteed unbreakable. Flaws in

castings (or even in hand forging) do occur and are not visible to the naked eye. If an iron or a bit, therefore, of a reliable metal breaks in fair use, then any saddler will exchange it for you and will take the matter up with the manufacturer. The percentage of such damage in proven metals is, however, very low indeed and, providing you buy the best available, you will be unlucky if you have trouble.

There is little or nothing you can do to prolong the life of bits and irons apart from normal cleaning; you can, however, take particular care of buckles. The tongue of a buckle is its weak spot, and care should be taken that this is greased when cleaning any item of tack so as to prevent corrosion, which can lead ultimately to a breakage.

THE BRIDLE

3

'It is not a question of learning how to use the reins but how to do without them'

In this chapter I intend to deal with the component parts of the bridle and, later, the methods by which the bridle is secured to the bit. Subsequent chapters deal with the action of various bits and with the principles involved in bitting.

Every type of bridle can be classified under one of five groups or families. These are:

(1) The Snaffle
(2) The Weymouth
(3) The Pelham
(4) The Gag
(5) The Bitless Bridle

The various parts of the bridle (Fig. 2) are common to all groups even if they do not take the same form. They are:

(1) The Head, in which is incorporated the throatlatch (pronounced, as is our English custom, throat*lash*). The throatlatch of the bridle is there to prevent the bridle slipping off the horse's head when emergencies arise, which might render this a possibility, and it should be so adjusted as to allow two fingers to be easily inserted between it and the animal's throat. A throatlatch adjusted too tightly throttles the horse and would effectively prevent your obtaining any degree of collection in the head carriage.

(2) The Cheeks, to which the bit is secured and which buckle on to the points of the head.

(3) The Browband or Front, as it is termed in the trade.

(4) The Cavesson or Noseband.

(5) The Reins.

In the case of the Double bridle the bradoon or snaffle is secured by a secondary strap and one cheekpiece (together known as the sliphead), which is passed through the slot of the browband. In a double bridle, the slot should be larger than in the snaffle bridle

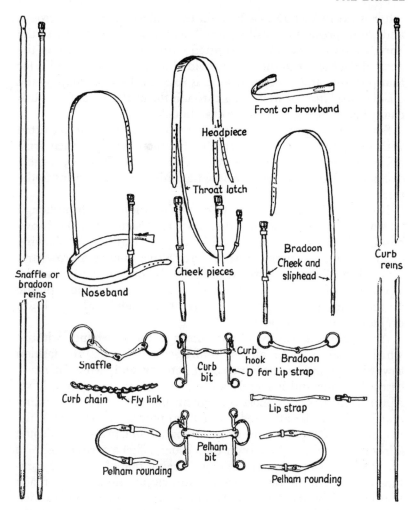

2. Parts of the bridle.

to allow for the extra thickness of this strap. The headstrap of the noseband is positioned last and therefore next to the animal. The cheek of the sliphead is fastened to the offside bit ring so that the buckle corresponds to that of the noseband head, which is fastened on the near side.

In both the Double bridle and the Pelham, two pairs of reins are used and there is the addition of a lipstrap. The purpose of the latter is (*a*) to keep the curb chain in its place in the curb groove and (*b*) to prevent a possible, if unlikely, reversal of the bit in the horse's mouth. The lipstrap is fitted with the buckle piece on the nearside of the bit in the loop provided on the cheek of the bit for that purpose, and the return strap is fixed in the same loop on the offside, this latter strap passing through the centre link of the curb chain before being attached to the buckle.

Some years ago it was fairly common to see a snaffle bit fitted with two pairs of reins, presumably for those who put their trust neither in princes nor in one rein. This practice has now largely disappeared and the snaffle bridle has only one pair of reins to the bit.

Now we will look at those parts of the bridle which, although serving the same basic purpose, vary in design. First the brow-band, which for hunting should be in plain leather. For showing or for racing, it is permissible and attractive to have a browband covered in silk or in plastic in the owner's colours. Plastic has the advantage of being easily cleaned, whereas silk has not; plastic in my opinion never looks so correct, though doubtless I am prejudiced in this respect.

An important feature of the bridle is the noseband, without which a horse looks almost undressed. It came into fashion towards the end of the nineteenth century and, while in many cases the noseband is merely an adornment, it is not entirely so. Apart from being the most convenient place to which a standing martingale can be attached—and I am now speaking only of the plain cavesson type, not the drop noseband—it can also, if adjusted fairly tightly and slightly lower than usual, effect a partial closure of the mouth, the opening of the mouth being one of the more common evasions of the bit. Obviously this closure does not approach that created by the drop noseband (the types and action of which are dealt with in the chapter 'Auxiliaries to the Action of the Bit'), as it is adjusted well up on the jaw-bones, but it can be helpful. If you intend to use a noseband in this way, it is better to inform the saddler lest he make the noseband without allowing for the necessary amount of adjustment.

The plain leather noseband is correct for hunting and I prefer it to be made as it is in the illustration (Fig. 2) with the headpiece slotted through the nosepiece and not sewn directly on to it. This ensures that the noseband does not droop or lose its shape and is also the only practical method to adopt when using a standing martingale. An ordinary stitched-on head will very quickly give way under the considerable strain imposed on it by a standing martingale, whereas the loop-through method will not.

For showing and racing the lighter and more elegant stitched noseband (Fig. 3) is popular and there is no reason why it should not appear on a hunting bridle also. It would, of course, be unwise to use a standing martingale with this type as it is not designed to withstand the possible strain.

For show jumping, where often a very tight (frequently too tight) standing martingale is used, imposing considerable pressure on both the noseband and the horse's nose, I would recommend a very stout noseband, padded with chamois round the nosepiece

3. Show noseband.

4. Sheepskin-covered noseband.

and possibly made of rawhide. Occasionally a rounded leather nosepiece is fitted to intensify this pressure on the nose when used in conjunction with a standing martingale. Again, if this device is really necessary, I would recommend that a thick piece of rounded rawhide or helvetia leather should be used in the nosepiece (not a thin one which might cut).

Last of all is the sheepskin-covered noseband (Fig. 4) made popular by French trainers and now a familiar sight on our racecourses, in show-jumping circles and, of all places, on children's ponies! It originated as an 'anti-shadow' or 'anti-shying' noseband for trotting horses in the United States and, in that sphere, I can see it has certain merits, which might possibly be extended to the racecourse providing the noseband is adjusted high enough up the face. Even so a surprising number of trainers hold divergent opinions as to its function. Personally I think its importance is exaggerated, although I admit it is a good way of spotting your horse if he happens to be the only animal running in one. For show jumping, if its aim is to prevent chafing, I would condone it; otherwise it is just another unnecessary appendage. For children's ponies it is both ridiculous and a needless expenditure.

THE REINS

Reins, to those who look upon them as life-lines, are an even more important item on the bridle. They are made in considerable variety with the object of giving a better grip. Apart from the normal plain leather rein, which in wet weather or on a sweating horse does become slippery, there is the *rubber*-covered rein. Invariably used for racing, frequently for show jumping, etc., and quite often in the hunting-field, too, it does afford an excellent grip. In this country the length of rubber is 30 in. and begins some 10 in. from the bit end of the rein. In America, where a much shorter hold is taken by race jockeys, the length of rubber is only 18 in. and it begins closer to the bit. Incidentally Americans seem to prefer a very much thicker rein for race riding than we do, the width often being as much as 1 in., whereas ⅝ in. for flat racing and ¾ in. for chasing are normal in this country.

There are two points to bear in mind when buying rubber reins. If they are to be used for chasing or point-to-pointing, particularly is it essential that there should be sufficient length in the buckle end of the handpart (all good-quality reins should have a buckle in the handpart and not be sewn together) for you to tie a knot so that in the event of your slipping the rein to its full extent, possibly when everything has gone wrong and you are performing extraordinary acrobatics to maintain some sort of affinity with your mount, you will not be exerting any undue pressure on the buckle fastening but rather on the knot and will thus avoid the disaster usually associated with the buckle fastening parting.

Secondly, the rubber covering should be stitched by hand with a large spot stitch down the centre of the rein it encloses. Close machine stitching may be quicker, but reduces the leather's strength with its line of close perforations. In time and with continued use the rubber handparts will wear smooth and will have to be replaced. This is not an unduly difficult job and any saddler should be able to undertake it for you.

Two reins somewhat similar in appearance and often confused

are the *plaited* rein and the *laced* rein. In the former the rein is split in strips, usually five, and then plaited, and in the latter a lace is inserted and passed over and through the reins in 'V'-shapes down its length. Both give excellent grip, but the plaited rein does tend to stretch; I once saw one that had attained the remarkable length of eight feet. Of the two I prefer the laced one, which has the added advantage that the labour involved in its making is less than that required for the plaited variety.

There are then a group of reins which are not made entirely from leather. Among these is the *web* rein, which is sometimes a tubular web, with or without finger slots of leather placed at intervals of four or five inches along the handpart; this is used with finger slots for show jumping and, when made of a plain, tough, ribbed web without finger slots, is a cheap and very hard-wearing exercise rein affording a good grip in all conditions. I am always surprised that it is not more popular, particularly among trainers who spend much time and money having rubber reins re-covered. Trainers are, however, notoriously conservative where tack is concerned. Also in this category are the ubiquitous, expensive and, to my mind, quite ineffectual *nylon-plaited* reins. Apart from being too long in most cases for their intended purpose—i.e. show jumping (a shorter rein to correspond with the usually shorter hold taken being desirable)—they achieve, when wet, a degree of slippery sliminess which is horrid and, when dry, become so hard and the edges so abrasive as to remove the skin from even the most calloused finger. You will gather that I do not approve of them and would put them well down my list of practical reins, although *linen*-corded reins do a reasonably effective job.

Very different is the 'Dartnall' rein made from soft plaited cotton, shaped to your hand in such a way that it lies most comfortably, and at the same time does not rub the hair from the horse's neck, a frequent occurrence with many other types of rein. They are named after their inventor, whose son still makes them not many miles from Richmond. They make a wonderful rein for jumping and, if you can afford it, for exercising too and in my opinion are among the finest reins ever made.

The length of a normal full size rein is 5 ft. or thereabouts; for show jumping, to conform with the shorter hold taken, 4 ft. 6 in.; and in the case of small children, 4 ft. 3 in. or shorter is quite sufficient as anything over that length hangs down where they can most easily catch their feet in the festoons of loop. The width will depend upon their own personal preference and upon the width of the bridle, the measurements of which are discussed later in this chapter. Normally, however big a front your horse may have, you will not get a leather rein to measure more than a little over 5 ft., for the simple reason that the back from which the rein is cut does not exceed that length, and it is unlikely that a breed of long-backed animals will be evolved purely to overcome this!

<h2 style="text-align:center">ATTACHMENT TO THE BIT</h2>

The next step to be considered in the making up of a bridle is concerned with its attachment to the bit.

There are five methods. First, the bridle can be sewn to the bit, which is invariably the case with a race bridle, a race exercise bridle and often with a showing bridle also. At one time this method was also *de rigueur* in the hunting-field, but times change and this is not now so. Nothing looks so neat as a *sewn* bridle and providing one takes proper care, it is safe. It does, however, have disadvantages. For one thing you cannot remove the bit when cleaning and it is important, therefore, to see that where the leather turns over the bit and where friction and consequently wear are greatest, it is kept well cleaned and greased to prevent the leather drying out and becoming brittle. Then again it is inconvenient for those who belong to the 'key to every horse's mouth' brigade and who find the key to be an elusive one. Constant changing of the bit in a sewn bridle is both bad for the bridle, the cutting out and restitching weakening the leather, and hard on the pocket in terms of labour costs.

Secondly, one can employ the now firmly established *stud* fastening, which can either be in the shape of a hook or a round stud. The fastening is always on the inside and looks neat and workmanlike. It is a joy to the searchers for the key and is nearly a hundred per cent safe, although I think I would personally prefer a sewn bridle if I were to ride in a steeplechase. Because the bridle is so easily dismantled the turns of leather where they come in contact with the metal of the bit can be regularly cleaned and so kept soft and supple. The danger in this fastening, if there is one, is that people will try to use force to fasten and more particularly unfasten these studs. The correct and easiest way to fasten a stud billet is to put the loose end round the bit ring, then pass it through the first keeper over the top of the stud, making no effort at this stage to push the stud through the slot, then well through the second keeper. Now press the leather in front of the stud down with your thumb and ease it in the reverse direction when the stud will slip into the slot. To undo the fastening, push the turn of leather encircling the bit ring forward again with one thumb, while the other thumb restrains the loose end. A loop will then be formed over the stud and it will slip out quite easily. On the whole, hook stud fastenings are among the more practical methods of attachment and have now found acceptance with all but the staunchest diehards.

A third method which one occasionally comes across is the *loop* fastening sometimes called 'monkey up the stick', a name which I find difficult to understand. This is generally found on show-jumping reins, and can also be seen on American and Australian racing reins. I have rarely seen this fastening on the bridle cheeks as well, but there is no reason why this should not be so as it is very convenient and workmanlike. It consists simply of a leather loop sewn on to the bit end of the cheek and rein, the actual loop being on the reverse side. Cheek and rein are then passed round the bit ring and through the loop to make a neat, secure and very safe fastening which is easily kept clean and supple. For an exercise bridle, either in a racing stable or otherwise, I think this rather neglected method would be admirable, and if one condones the hook stud for hunting bridles, then I see no reason why the more easily made loop fastening should not also be equally acceptable.

Another fastening now seldom seen is the *snap billet* type (Fig. 5), employed by Count Robert Orssich for showing bridles. This consists of a neat snap billet or hook set into the leather of the cheeks and reins and clipped on to the bits. Undoubtedly it is very neat and unobtrusive and the fact that we have metal moving against metal and not against leather does improve the free action of the bits. It is, however, limited in its application to show bridles only and it would be inadvisable, if not dangerous, to use it for hunting or indeed any other form of horse activity. The trouble is, of course, that the hooks can be so easily overstrained when putting them on to the bits that, once forced, they become unsafe.

Even if you are very careful with these hooks, it is still advisable to know that your horse is not going to take off with you, otherwise you will find yourself in the same predicament as the lady who some years ago showed an ex-racehorse at one of the principal shows in just such a bridle. It was a class for hacks and the race-horse, having begun his canter sedately enough, decided to enliven the proceedings by showing how fast he could go if he really tried. Horse and rider careered round the ring both pulling hard until such time as the little snap billets had had enough and, on their giving up the unequal struggle, the bits just fell out of the mouth. Fortunately, the horse was stopped and no great harm was done. Many showing stars do use them quite satisfactorily, but I would not recommend them to a novice.

I have purposely left the *buckle* fastening to the last because as a means of attachment it is in that order also that I would employ it. Buckles are to my eye incorrect and can, by their propensity for getting caught up in almost anything that is to hand, be dangerous also. In addition, most cheap bridles tend to go in for this type of fastening and a man who makes or sells a cheap bridle is naturally going to use a cheap buckle. Buckles have tongues, and cheap buckles have tongues which bend, corrode and ultimately break. I would excuse a strong buckle on a stout exercise bridle, but under no other circumstances. The American market does call for a buckle on its race bridles and these are usually very strong and well made, but even so they spoil what to my mind is an otherwise eminently practical article.

On the subject of buckles, which form a part of all bridles, and the weakest part at that, two types will be found—a square buckle which I personally prefer, or a rounded buckle, known as a 'fiddle' buckle. Providing they are the best obtainable—and the only way to ensure this is to buy a bridle of top merit from a reputable firm—a user will find little difference between the two. I do think, however, that the square buckle follows the shape of the point better, whereas the 'fiddle' tends to pinch the edges of the leather, but it is really a matter of individual preference.

BRIDLES AND THEIR SCOPE

This is an appropriate place in which to mention the differences between bridles and the scope of each. I would divide them into Hunting (show jumping, cross-country, etc.), Showing and Racing, and Exercising.

Hunting bridles should be made from leather having plenty of substance and the width of the cheek will probably be $\frac{3}{4}$ in. with the rein, of whichever type you prefer, either the same width or a little wider. In a double bridle or a Pelham where two reins are employed, the bradoon or snaffle rein will be $\frac{1}{8}$ in. wider than the curb rein. An ordinary hunting bridle has reins of $\frac{3}{4}$ in. and $\frac{5}{8}$ in. respectively.

A show bridle, particularly in hack and pony classes, will be a lighter affair altogether and will be made from leather of a thinner substance. In this case the width of the cheek may well be $\frac{5}{8}$ in. or even $\frac{1}{2}$ in. with correspondingly narrow reins.

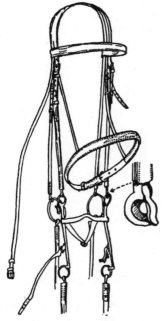

5. Snap billet type bridle.

Many showing people, particularly in pony classes, demand reins so thin that after a little use they must assume an appearance similar to that of a bootlace. While I appreciate that a child may find a thick rein difficult to hold, it is as well to remember that too thin a rein encourages clenching of the hand, and with the consequent tightening of the forearm muscles, it becomes easy for the child (or adult) to develop a pair of 'mutton-fists'.

Racing men are obsessed with the idea of weight, as indeed they have to be, with jockeys having to count every ounce, and race bridles, particularly flat-race bridles, are therefore very light, the

33

cheek not exceeding $\frac{1}{2}$ in. in width and the reins (rubber hand-parted) $\frac{5}{8}$ in.

Chasing bridles are stouter, with a $\frac{5}{8}$-in. or $\frac{3}{4}$-in. cheek and a $\frac{3}{4}$-in. rein, unless, of course, the owner has a particular preference for a wider rein.

Exercising bridles alternatively should be stout and of good substance. The tougher the better, for race-exercise bridles get more rough treatment than any other form of bridle, and they can

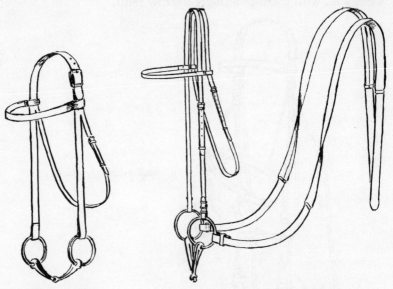

6. *'Dealer's' bridle.*   7. *American pattern bridle.*

either be sewn, or possibly fastened, to the bit by the loop method. A good type of exercise bridle is the old 'dealer's' bridle (Fig. 6), with a single buckle adjustment on the poll. I have often wondered why they are not more in demand with trainers, as they are certainly cheaper and I would have thought more practical where labour is such that tack is the last thing to get cleaned.

I have always admired the American pattern bridle (Fig. 7) and, although its appearance may seem a little odd, it is undeniably strong and has so much adjustment that it would be difficult to find a horse it would not fit. The bridle is always double-sewn, sometimes being lined with rawhide and the head and the throat-latch are made separately, being joined by three double loops. A noseband is not usually worn with this bridle. My illustration shows a buckle fastening, but the bridle would be an ideal subject for a loop-type fastening.

Bridles are usually made in three general sizes: Pony, Cob and Full Size. Personally I find these names annoying and confusing as there are numbers of ponies with enormous heads that would never fit into a pony bridle, and 'cob' is an extremely vague term covering too great a multitude of equine sins. However, as a general guide they will continue to be referred to thus. Personally, I would much rather know the size and type of pony and, if in doubt, have a measurement taken from lip to lip over the poll.

Bit sizes can also cause difficulty, and when measuring a bit with a straight mouth—that is, an unjointed one—the measurement taken should be the inside measurement between the cheeks or the rings. For a jointed bit measure it between the rings laid flat. As a rough guide the inside measurement of a Weymouth or Pelham bit corresponds to the size of animal as follows:

$5\frac{1}{2}$ in. = Full-size hunter.
$5\frac{1}{4}$ in. = Blood horse or between 15 h.h. and 16 h.h.
5 in. = 14·2 h.h.–15 h.h.
$4\frac{3}{4}$ in. = 13·2 h.h.–14·2 h.h.
$4\frac{1}{2}$ in. = 12 h.h.–13 h.h.

It is interesting to note that bit sizes have decreased by inches during the past century. Bits with 7-in. and even 8-in. mouths were at one time quite common. Today with so much more thoroughbred blood having played its part in evolving a finer bred horse, $5\frac{1}{2}$ in. is rarely exceeded.

4 | THE PRINCIPLES AND MECHANICS OF BITTING

'Half of riding is seat, the other half is legs'

In this chapter we shall consider the basic action of each of our five families of bridles upon those parts of the horse's head on which pressure is exerted. The action of various differently shaped members of these families is discussed in later chapters.

We should, before thinking of the mechanics of bitting, appreciate that while the bit *assists* us in positioning the head in such a way as to give us maximum control over the speed and direction we wish to assume, it is not in itself the *originator* but rather the *extension* of the process.

The origin of the head position lies in the early training of the horse, which should induce suppleness of poll, neck and spine, thus enabling the motive power of the horse—the loins and the hocks—to become engaged. The bit is the last item in the chain and to attempt to obtain any form of advanced head carriage by the agency of the bit alone results only in stiffness and a restricted action. The motive force, which is behind the saddle, is controlled by the application of our legs and seat, and the bit, through the agency of our hand, becomes an extension of these forces.

It is nevertheless essential that even if we appreciate and practise these concepts, and more particularly if we don't, that we should understand the action of the bits we use.

We have seen in the previous chapter that all bits or systems of bitting can be grouped into one of five families. These are:

(1) The Snaffle (Fig. 8).
(2) The Weymouth or Double bridle (Fig. 9).
(3) The Pelham (Figs. 10 and 11).
(4) The Gag (Fig. 12).
(5) The Bitless bridle (Fig. 13).

Occasionally we shall find marriages between the families, resulting in a part combination of the characteristics of two, or we shall find one whose construction has been altered to accentuate a particular characteristic, but basically all types can be so divided.

All these groups impose control by operating on one or more of the seven parts of the horse's head upon which pressure is applied by the bit. The seven parts are:

(1) The corners of the mouth.
(2) The bars of the mouth.
(3) The tongue.
(4) The poll.
(5) The curb groove.
(6) The nose.
(7) The roof of the mouth.

Martingales and nosebands, particularly those of the drop variety, are, when used, an integral part of bitting, and being auxiliaries to the bit, either intensify and/or alter its action. For this reason they are included in the series of chapters connected with bitting.

THE SNAFFLE

The snaffle family, consisting of one mouthpiece either jointed in the centre or unjointed in a half-moon shape known as a mullen

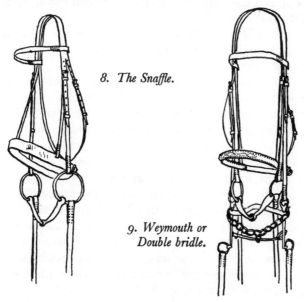

8. *The Snaffle.*

9. *Weymouth or Double bridle.*

mouth, is the simplest form of bridle, and in both cases the movement is an upward, head-raising one acting on the corners of the mouth. The jointed mouthpiece produces a squeezing or nutcracker movement on the mouth, which is lacking in the mullen mouth variety, making it more severe than the latter. In the mullen mouthpiece a slight bearing is taken upon the tongue, as is the case with all such mouthpieces.

As a general rule little flexion of either the poll or the lower jaw can be obtained with this bit. The addition of a dropped noseband, however, changes the character of the snaffle as we see when we discuss this particular auxiliary.

THE WEYMOUTH

The Weymouth or Double bridle (in this latter designation I include any type of curb bit used in conjunction with a bradoon), contrary to the snaffle, is the most advanced form of bitting and employs many more of our seven parts of the head to achieve its object. Because it is the most advanced bridle, its use should be confined—and it is not always so—to the educated horseman and to the horse who has reached a more advanced stage of training. The bridle consists of the bradoon or snaffle below which in the mouth is placed the curb bit fitted with a curb chain, thus giving us two bits in the mouth.

The bradoon is normally a jointed one and the mouthpiece of the curb is a straight bar, in the centre of which is an upward bend known as the port.

In this bridle the correct positioning of the head is achieved by (a) raising the head with the snaffle by upward pressure on the corners of the mouth and (b) by lowering the head and bringing the nose inwards to a position a little in advance of the vertical by means of the curb bit. To achieve this positioning, the curb operates first on the bars of the mouth (the port in the mouthpiece, allowing room for the tongue and removing pressure from it, enables the mouthpiece on either side of the port to bear downwards on to the bars of the mouth). The degree of this bearing on the bars depends accordingly upon the size and shape of the port. A mullen (half-moon) mouthpiece in a curb bit would transfer the pressure from the bars to the tongue and, conversely, a deep and wide port would allow greater bearing surface on the bars by allowing more room for the tongue.

Secondly, the curb bit operates on the poll by means of an increased downward tension on the cheekpieces of the bridle when sufficient feel on the curb rein places the cheek of the bit at an angle of 45 degrees or more.

Finally, on assuming this angle the curb chain tightens in the curb groove, applying a downward and backward pressure on the lower jaw.

In a curb bit where the port was unusually high, the last of the seven parts—the roof of the mouth—would be brought into play and the increased leverage would intensify the downward force. Fortunately such bits are rarely found today and the use of the roof of the mouth to assist in obtaining the correct head carriage would not normally be regarded as legitimate or humane.

Given a horse then whose elementary training in the snaffle has been properly carried out and a rider of equal calibre, the combination of forces brought into play by this bridle will result in the production of a head carriage most conducive to maximum control. The head will thus be carried fairly high with the nose in advance of the vertical and the poll and lower jaw bending and relaxing in accordance with the indication of the hand. From the opposite viewpoint it requires no great flight of imagination to envisage the damage and discomfort that could be caused by the inexpert horseman.

In this country it is usual for the bradoon rein to be held on the outside of the little finger and outside the curb rein, thereby accentuating the action of the bradoon. Mr Henry Wynmalen, however, in his book, *Equitation* (Country Life), recommends the French way whereby the bradoon rein is held between the third and fourth finger and the curb rein under the little finger, with consequently more emphasis on the curb bit than on the bradoon. As in this position the reins are held to correspond with the position of the bradoon and the bit in the mouth, this would seem to be logical, and certainly many well-known instructors including Mrs Lisa Shedden, who trained with Cuyer, advocate this method. It is only fair to say, however, that there are others who use the former method equally successfully.

THE PELHAM

Our third group of bridles is the Pelham, which is a half-way house between the snaffle and the double bridle. It tries to achieve the same result as the double bridle, but with the employment of only one mouthpiece. Theoretically, and I believe practically also, this is impossible; nevertheless, it is a useful bit in which many animals go exceedingly well. Its success is probably due to the fact that it is a sloppy, kind bit which many horses seem to appreciate. In its most common form the mouthpiece is a mullen one of either metal or vulcanite, but there are numerous variations, discussed later, by which its action is changed.

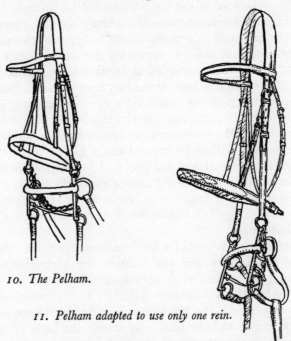

10. The Pelham.

11. Pelham adapted to use only one rein.

Generally speaking, however, the Pelham's action is achieved by pressure on the corners of the mouth when the snaffle rein predominates, and on the poll and curb groove when the curb rein is the stronger. When a mullen mouthpiece is used, pressure is upon the tongue and not on the bars. Inevitably these pressures are ill defined and its action can never be the positive one of the double bridle. In this, too, may lie part of its success. The reference to the position of the reins in the hands made in connection with the double bridle is likewise applicable to this bit.

In addition, the Pelham will often be seen used, particularly by children, with a leather rounding or couple joining the snaffle ring to the curb ring so that one rein only, attached to this coupling, is employed (Figs. 2 and 11). Apart from the fact that one rein for children is easier to manage than two, I have never been able to make sense of this device. If the leather of the rounding and the turn of the rein around it is well greased, and it usually is not, and if the rounding is as short in length as possible, and it rarely is, then I will concede that with a lowered hand the rein will move slightly down the rounding and some curb and poll pressure will be induced. On the other hand, if these conditions are not fulfilled, I cannot see that any very positive action is likely to ensue.

Worse than the roundings, which do allow a little action, is the now fortunately uncommon divided rein. This is a rein which begins as two reins attached one to the snaffle ring and one to the bit ring and is then joined into one single rein some eighteen inches from the bit. This I just do not comprehend. Apart from the convenience of one rein in the child's hand, there would appear to be no good reason for using a Pelham bit in this fashion. There are other bits which will give the child more effective control if that is what is required.

THE GAG

The fourth group is the Gag family. Really an exaggerated snaffle; the rings of the bit have holes set in them at top and bottom and through these rings is passed a cheekpiece of rounded leather to which the rein is attached. The upward head-raising action is, therefore, accentuated by the rounding sliding through the holes in the bit ring, the action thus becoming a clear indication to the horse that he should raise his head smartly.

This bridle is of particular use on those unpleasant animals who persist in approaching their fences at great speed and with their noses held uncomfortably close to ground level. Logically, of course, one can argue that the gag might also lower the head because you cannot exert an upward pressure on the corners of the mouth in this way without a consequent downward pressure being brought to bear on the poll. It is, therefore, something of a contradiction in opposing forces with the head, between the poll and the corners of the mouth, being compressed between them. However, for practical purposes we can assume that the gag does raise the head, although continued and inexpert use will result in a very stiff head carriage.

In this respect it is always advisable to have two reins on a gag bridle, the one connected to the rounded cheekpieces and the other attached to the ring itself in the normal way. The horse can then be ridden on the latter while he is carrying his head correctly and the former need be brought into play only as the necessity arises. Used in this fashion the gag remains an effective instrument, whereas continual riding on the gag rein alone will lead to a stiffened head carriage and may ultimately result in the horse finding further evasions.

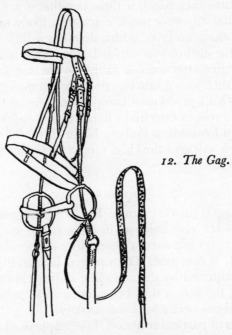

12. The Gag.

A gag with a small ring, such as the Cheltenham, or a Duncan gag, is sometimes used to replace the bradoon of a double bridle, thereby accentuating the upward action of this article, and occasionally one will see a sharp twisted gag of the overcheck variety in use.

The rounded cheekpieces of a gag bridle are made of leather rounded on to a piece of cord and while the initial appearance is good, the constant friction with the metal of the bit ring causes wear in a very short time. I would much prefer to use a strip of buffalo hide or helvetia very well greased, which would last far longer even though its appearance might not be so good. In any case, of course, it is essential that the rounding should be kept well greased to assist the sliding action.

THE BITLESS

The last of our bridle groups is that known as Bitless and it relies upon our one remaining part of the head to achieve control—i.e. the nose. As its name implies, it is not concerned with the mouth

13. The Bitless bridle

at all and therein lies its strength. Most varieties of bitless bridles combine pressure on the nose with pressure on the curb groove, and in Blair's pattern (Fig. 13), one of the most common, the cheekpieces, although not nearly so long as in the old Hackamores, are sufficiently long to give considerable leverage. Other patterns are made without cheeks of this type and the simplest 'do-it-yourself' variety would be a drop noseband with a couple of rings on it to which the reins could be attached.

The various types of bitless bridles are discussed in more detail in the chapter devoted to them, but their advantages can be clearly seen when dealing with a horse whose mouth has sustained so much damage as to render the use of a bit impractical, or with a horse who through bad management will not go well in any normal bridle.

While a horse can safely be ridden in these bridles (their stopping power is more than ample), it is obvious that school movements and particularly anything calling for lateral work would not be within their scope.

To conclude this chapter, one or two general observations might be helpful. The first of these concerns the thickness of the mouthpiece in any bit; as a rule it is true to say that a broad thick mouthpiece is more comfortable for the horse and gives to the rider greater control. A thin mouthpiece concentrates the pressure on a small area and bad hands will quickly remove all sense of feeling from the affected parts, resulting in a dead mouth or in a horse who cannot be stopped— probably both. Horses pull *against* pain and a sharp bit encourages this practice. A broad mouthpiece is softer in its action and spreads its pressure over a larger area of sensory nerves, the resultant comfort experienced by the horse rendering him more amenable to control.

Mouthpieces of rubber or, if this is too mild, vulcanite, are all relatively thick and are kind to the mouth. The practice of some trainers of covering a bit with soft leather on either side of the mouthpiece is also conducive to comfort. It is a mistaken kindness that rejects a broad-mouthed bit for a narrow pencil of a mouthpiece on the grounds that it is too heavy for the horse to carry comfortably. The horse has more than enough strength in its head and neck to carry the additional ounce or so involved.

Secondly, it will not require any great thought to realise that in the case of curb bits (including Pelhams) the degree of severity will depend upon the length of the cheek, a long cheek giving considerably more leverage than a short one.

SEGUNDO'S SYSTEM OF BITTING

It is interesting to observe that as long ago as 1832 one Juan Segundo produced a system of bitting which, although entirely mechanical, was meticulous in its study of these seven parts of the head and the action of various shaped mouthpieces upon them. Segundo in his study of the horse's mouth divided horses into six groups: very hard mouthed, hard mouthed, good mouthed, etc., basing his classification to some extent on the size and shape of the bars and tongue—that is, a horse with broad, flat and heavily fleshed bars would be hard mouthed, and one with sharply accentuated lightly covered bars would be soft mouthed. He produced six curb bits with varied mouthpieces and length and shape of cheeks to be used with a combination of curb chains, which he claimed as a panacea of all equine bitting problems.

His system never achieved success in this country, although many highly coloured letters praising it appeared in his treatise over the names of various continental cavalry commanders of the period.

Today, apart from a purely mechanical standpoint, his bits would be considered severe and much of his theory and recommendations as to the mouthpiece best suited to accommodate the tongue would be questioned. There are, however, still a few Segundo bits (Fig. 14) used in this country at the present time.

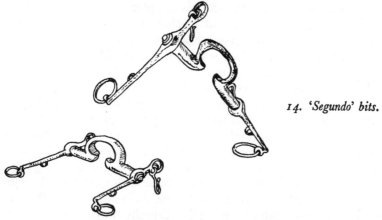

14. 'Segundo' bits.

I know that Mr G. R. Rudkin, until recently manager of Woolmers Park Polo Club and a most knowledgeable man in this field, keeps one or two by him and finds them useful in certain cases. The removal of the tongue into the heart-shaped port allows a very definite bearing on the bars, but demands excellent hands.

The treatise was included in what is believed to be the only loriner's book published. This book, entitled *The Loriner* (a maker of bridle bits), was produced with a large number of illustrations by Benjamin Latchford in 1883 (Latchford was a famous loriner with premises in London) and the well-known saying 'There is a key to every horse's mouth' originated from a passage in his book. Personally, I would rather think of the key as lying not only in the bit but in the training of the horse and in the application of the rider's seat, legs and hands as well. I am also very fond of quoting another of his assertions that of every twenty bits he made, nineteen were for men's heads and one for the horse's!

5 | AUXILIARIES TO THE ACTION OF THE BIT

'It takes two to pull'

In the last chapter I mentioned that nosebands and martingales must be regarded as auxiliaries to the bit, emphasising and sometimes changing its action. In this chapter I want to deal with these auxiliaries in detail and to show the ways in which they assist, and in some cases counteract certain evasions, by helping the bit to position the head where we require it so that the horse becomes more obedient to our hand.

There has recently been considerable controversy in the horse world over the use of many of these auxiliaries. Most of it has centred on one or two of the martingales and that old bone of contention, the drop noseband, and the show-jumping fraternity are in the centre of target. I would never condone cruelty and I will admit that in one or two instances the number of gadgets adorning a show-jumper's head has been nothing short of horrific, and yet it would be wrong to blame the majority for the sake of one or two blatant offenders. Equally would it be wrong to censure either the drop noseband or any of the martingales as such; it is the misuse of these articles that lays them open to criticism, not the articles themselves. It is even worse in my opinion to malign these perfectly legitimate auxiliaries in print, as some do, when the writers' very approach indicates that they have little or no knowledge of the action of the article about which they are getting so irate. Obviously the ideal would be to produce a horse in such a state of training and of such conformation as to render the use of extraneous paraphernalia unnecessary, but the fact is that very few horses are so educated and it is probable that only a small percentage of people could ride them if they were.

Whatever the reasons for this state of affairs and however much one may deplore them (after all there are thousands of people quite happy to sit on a horse without worrying their heads about the position of any part of either their own or the horse's anatomy—and good luck to them!), it is still true that they, and others in more competitive spheres, find it necessary on this account, in order to preserve control and their own safety, to employ some form of auxiliary. Under these circumstances and providing that the horse is allowed the maximum freedom compatible with comfort, I can see no cruelty in their use.

THE DROP NOSEBAND

Let us first consider the drop noseband, of which there are a number of patterns. All of them succeed in closing the mouth (opening of the mouth or crossing of the jaws, thereby sliding the bit through the mouth and so avoiding the correct action, being common evasions). Even more important is the fact that the drop noseband, used in conjunction with a snaffle, alters the whole conception of the snaffle bit. The noseband imposes pressure on the nose, following pressure on the bit through the reins, and the resultant position of the head (i.e. lowered because of the nose pressure) allows the bit to come more into contact with the bars, exerting again a downward and inward force as opposed to the normal upward pull when the bit is acting purely on the corners of the mouth. Briefly, therefore, it is possible to produce very adequate flexion of the lower jaw and the poll, not normally possible with the snaffle alone. The drop noseband, by positioning the head correctly, materially assists the rider's control, and although it qualifies as an accessory to the bit, it has its own place in the training of the horse. Correctly adjusted it is a far better thing and far less damaging than the double bridle put on a horse too early in its education, by people who use double bridles for the not very sensible reason of always having done so.

The correct fitting for the drop noseband (Fig. 15) is for the nosepiece, which should be broad enough to avoid intense localised pressure, to lie some $2\frac{1}{2}$ in. to 3 in. above the nostrils just below the termination of the facial bones, with the rear strap fastening under the bit and lying in the curb groove. It should fit snugly but not excessively tightly and thus should have no detrimental effect upon the wind. In fact, an overbent horse (i.e. with his nose on his chest), made so by the misuse of a double bridle, is far more likely to be affected in his breathing.

The important thing when buying a dropped noseband is to make sure that the nosepiece is fixed in such a way that it cannot drop downwards over the nostrils. This is done by either the use of a ring which has two projecting spikes which are sewn into the nosepiece and the head strap, or by a connecting cross-piece of leather from the base of the head to the nosepiece or by both.

OTHER TYPES OF NOSEBAND

Obviously it would be stupid and cruel to attach a standing martingale to a drop noseband and, if it is necessary to use both, a Flash noseband (Fig. 16) will be the answer. This is really just a

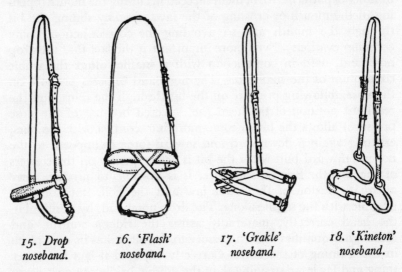

| *15. Drop noseband.* | *16. 'Flash' noseband.* | *17. 'Grakle' noseband.* | *18. 'Kineton' noseband.* |

strong cavesson noseband with the addition of two crossing straps sewn to the centre of the nosepiece, which are fastened below the bit and achieve much the same result, although the point of pressure on the nose is a little higher than on the drop noseband. The standing martingale can then be fitted to the cavesson in the usual way.

The Grakle noseband (Fig. 17), named after a Grand National winner who wore one, has the lower straps fastened under the bit and the top ones above, with a connection at the rear to keep them in place. The nose pressure in this case is localised at the point where the straps intersect and is possibly stronger than the normal drop, while allowing a little more movement in the jaws. It can, however, be adjusted so that the pressure point is a little higher than usual. It is useful for hard-pulling horses and those that delight in crossing their jaws.

In recent years the Grakle has been called the figure eight or the cross-over noseband, but these latter were not really shaped like the Grakle, although at the present time there is precious little difference between them.

The Kineton or Puckle noseband (Fig. 18) is named after its inventor who lived at Kineton and is worth having in any stable specialising in hard pullers, for its action is fairly severe and it is essentially designed for use with this particular type of horse. It differs from other members of the drop noseband group in that

19. 'Bucephalus' noseband.

it does not close the mouth and consists of two metal loops with a connecting nose strap which is adjustable at both ends. The centre of the nosepiece is usually reinforced with a strip of light metal covered with leather, the loops being fitted on the inside of the bit rings and behind the mouthpiece. Pressure on the bit and its consequent movement to the rear is then transmitted to the nose, effecting a lowering of the head. The noseband should be adjusted so that the loops are in contact with the bit and it follows that the tighter the nosepiece is adjusted, the more salutary will be its effect upon the nose. Without doubt the Kineton is almost a 'last hope' device which should be confined to confirmed tearaways. It occasionally appears on the racecourse; not during the actual race itself but when the horse is going down to the post and it is removed before the 'off'.

A noseband now somewhat out of fashion is the Bucephalus (Fig. 19), although I believe Colonel Talbot-Ponsonby has one or two. It is also known as the Jobey noseband and is for use with either a Pelham or the curb bit of a double bridle. It is just a swelled and padded strap tapering at the ends to a small dee. At the centre of the nosepiece is a small buckle and strap for securing it to the cavesson noseband, the ends then passing round the jaws so that the offside dee fastens on to the nearside curb hook of the bit and the nearside dee to the offside curb hook. In this way a further pressure point—that of the nose—is added to those already employed by the curb bit.

As I have mentioned in Chapter 3, an ordinary cavesson noseband adjusted a hole or two lower than usual and fastened tight will have the effect of both closing the mouth and lowering the head, but clearly the action is not so well defined as that of the drop noseband.

MARTINGALES

The purpose of martingales in all cases is to achieve a lowering of the head thereby giving the rider more control by preventing evasion of the bit, which would occur if the head were thrown up. In the negotiation of any obstacle it is desirable, and much safer, if the horse's head is held low and the neck stretched; he then jumps with a rounded supple back and, although when racing at speed the parabola of the leap may be flatter, in jumping any obstacle at any speed, a head flung up high with the consequent stiffening and hollowing of the back would result in the horse hitting the fence with unpleasant results.

The purist will say that the horse's early training should make him sufficiently supple in his neck and back so that there is no need for any contrivance to get his head down—and he is undoubtedly right. Unfortunately, we return again to the fact that horses are not always so trained and also that some of them, who may well be good performers, have their heads and necks so placed on their bodies as to make it difficult if not dangerous to ride them without some form of martingale.

The most common form of martingale is the *standing* one, sometimes called a 'fast' martingale, and it is simplest in its action. It consists in basic form of a leather body with a loop at either end, one of which fastens on to the girth through the forelegs and the other on to the noseband. In common with all martingales, it has a neck strap to keep it in position and possibly to act as a lifeline for those with insecure seats.

The downward force it exerts on the nose achieves its object of keeping the head down. Clearly the tighter the martingale the greater is the control obtained, but it is occasionally abused by being adjusted so tightly that the horse loses all freedom of his neck; while this position gives the rider more control, it must affect the animal's powers of extension. For to jump well, particularly over spread fences, the animal must be able to stretch his head and neck. Adjusted to a reasonable length it does not affect the animal's jumping capacity, for a horse does not require to throw his head and neck up when he jumps (if he does, he should be stopped quickly) but rather to stretch them outwards and downwards.

The type of standing martingale I prefer is one with a buckle adjustment at the top (Fig. 20) rather than at the girth, and, if it is to be used for show jumping or polo, I like the top strap to be lined with rawhide and fastened with a stout buckle. This pattern is far easier to fit correctly than the one where the adjustment is on the loop to the girth.

An interesting mixture of noseband and martingale is the Grainger pattern (Fig. 21) where the martingale is directly and permanently attached to the noseband, this being adjusted midway between the positions adopted by the drop noseband and the ordinary cavesson, pressure being consequently more upon the nose than is usual. Captain Fergus Sutherland, a great man across a country, uses this device on very strong horses often in conjunction with a gag bridle (this aspect of the gag is discussed in the chapter devoted to the gag). The sliding fitment on the two branches of the martingale can be altered to make the pressure on the nose-piece either more or less severe. I can appreciate that a horse so tied down would be more amenable to discipline, but I would hold that his powers of extension over spread fences must necessarily be restricted as a result.

Years ago when show jumping was somewhat different, a popular variant was a standing martingale fitted with a quick-release device situated at the breast and operated by pulling a leather tag, a performance which could be achieved without dismounting. On release of the device, the martingale, until then pretty tight, could be lengthened by some six inches, the idea being that, after having cleared the upright fences with head well tied down and at whatever pace you liked, you extended the martingale in order to give the horse more freedom when you set sail at the water-jump, which was usually the last fence. With the change in show-jumping rules and methods (that mad gallop at the water was never necessary and rarely successful), the quick-release martingale became obsolete.

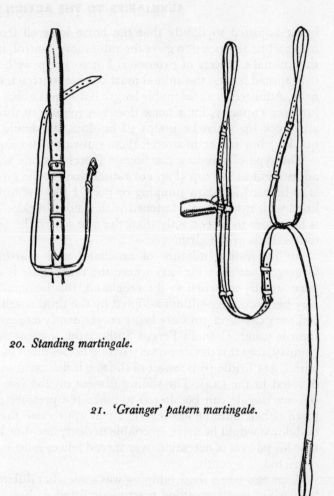

20. Standing martingale.

21. 'Grainger' pattern martingale.

Another variation, which has also largely disappeared, is the standing martingale made to fasten on to a ring on the cavesson with a stout snap hook incorporating a coiled spring. The spring allowed an inch or two of 'give' in the otherwise rigid martingale and for this reason I think it is a pity it should have gone out of fashion.

The running martingale (Fig. 22) is a little more complex in its action, the reins being passed through the rings of the martingale, and restraint being imposed on the mouth when the horse raises his head beyond the limit allowed him by the adjustment of the martingale. It will be clear that the tighter this is, the greater will be the restriction on the upward movement of the head and the greater the rider's control. If the martingale is so tight as to make the rein form an angle between the mouth and the hand, its action, particularly with a jointed snaffle, will be severe. The basic action of the snaffle is again altered by the downward pull which brings

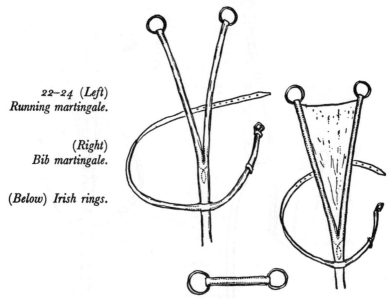

22–24 (Left)
Running martingale.

(Right)
Bib martingale.

(Below) Irish rings.

the bearing of the bit more on to the bars and away from the corners of the mouth.

Properly adjusted (the rings of the martingale in a line with the withers), it is, I believe, a help to people with not so good hands, but if the adjustment is tight and low then good hands are very necessary if the horse is to be comfortable.

The bib martingale (Fig. 23) comes within the province of the racehorse trainer, the centre-piece of leather between the branches being a sensible safety precaution against an excited horse getting himself caught up or even getting his nose between the branches. Its action is otherwise exactly that of the running martingale, though no trainer would ever have it as tightly adjusted as one occasionally sees in the show-jumping ring.

Irish rings (Fig. 24) are again a racing requisite and although sometimes called Irish martingales, they have no effect upon the positioning of the head, their use being confined to assisting the correct direction of the rein pull and to prevent the rein coming right over the head in the case of a fall.

If a running martingale is used, an essential safety precaution is a pair of rein stops, which consist of pieces of leather with slots in

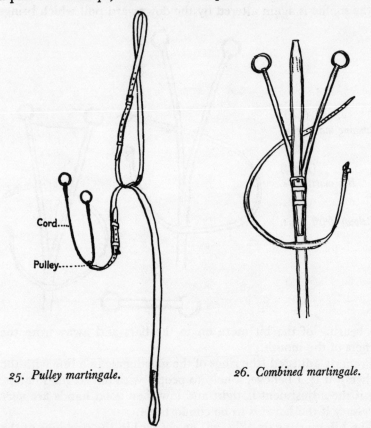

Cord....

Pulley.......

25. Pulley martingale.   *26. Combined martingale.*

the centre slid down the reins and possibly stitched some 10 in. from the bit. These will prevent the rings of the martingale sliding forward and perhaps getting caught in either the rein fastening or even over a tooth. Nothing will put a horse so quickly into reverse gear as this!

A pattern of running martingale which I feel is unjustly neglected is the pulley martingale (Fig. 25) where the rings are set on a cord which passes through a pulley at the top of the body. Mrs Lisa Shedden, whose approach to any horse problem is invariably sound, has used this martingale for many years, and I can only think that it is because people do not know about it that it is not more popular. Its advantage is that for lateral movement of the head and the quick changes of direction required in modern jumping, it allows the horse to bend his head and neck in the required direction without the restriction against the opposite side of his mouth (i.e. the offside when making a left-handed turn and contrariwise), which must be exerted with an ordinary running martingale. The unrestricted up and down movement of the rings through the pulley must accommodate themselves according to the position of either rein without putting unwanted pressure on either side when turning sharply.

For the show jumpers a combined martingale (Fig. 26) does, as the name suggests, combine both running and standing martingale in one and has the action of both.

If a running martingale is used with a double bridle (whether it should be or not is a matter of opinion) one either requires a smaller ring or, more satisfactorily, what is known as a triangle fitting with a roller which runs on the rein without either twisting it or getting caught up. At the same time, bearing in mind the action of a double bridle—i.e. the bradoon raising the head and the curb lowering it—the running martingale should be affixed in its logical place on the curb rein to assist the lowering action, which is the object of both the martingale and the curb bit. A martingale designed to lower the head put on to the bradoon rein, which is used to raise the head, is an illogical contradiction.

The last martingale I intend to discuss as an auxiliary is the much-maligned Market Harborough (Fig. 27), which in slightly different forms, all employing the same principle, is sometimes known, incorrectly, as the German rein. In Germany it is known as the 'English' rein! I class this as a martingale rather than as a rein because its action is primarily that of this group. Basically, it is a usual martingale body which ends at the breast in a ring to which are attached two strips of either rawhide or rounded leather, the former being the more satisfactory. These two strips pass upwards through the ring of the bit, are then connected to an otherwise normal rein with an adjusting buckle, or more satisfactorily with a small snap hook sewn to the end of the strip, and thence fastened on to one or other of four metal dees sewn along the actual rein. Either method allows one the necessary adjustment required to impose more or less restriction on the upward movement of the head.

The action is a simple one and is operated not by the rider's hand, but by the horse's head. While the horse carries his head

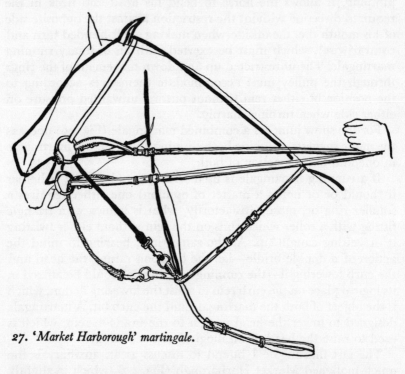

27. 'Market Harborough' martingale.

correctly, the strips passing through the bit rings are slack and inoperative; they tighten and exert their downward pull on the bit, and consequently on the bars of the mouth, only when the head is thrown upwards. There is absolutely no restriction on the extension of head and neck while jumping, and it is extremely good on a headstrong horse.

The Market Harborough, or anything else you like to call it, is in reality an improvement on the old draw rein which was fastened to the girth on either side, passing through the rings of the bit and back to the rider's hand. Its effect, in all but the most expert hands, was to produce an overbent horse whose powers of extension were naturally limited. Why the Market Harborough should receive so much abuse I do not understand, as it cannot be any more harmful than either a running or standing martingale, and is considerably less severe than the former when that article is tightly adjusted and used perhaps with a twisted snaffle.

A further variation of the Market Harborough borrows something from the De Gogue, discussed in a later chapter, and combines a piece of rounded leather running from the rein through a pulley fixed just below the ear and then back through the bit ring to a dee on the rein. This type employs, of course, poll pressure as well to induce the lowering of the head.

Used sensibly, all these auxiliaries can assist us in the riding of our horses and in their training, and providing we think of them as means to an end and not an end in themselves, we shall be putting them in their true perspective.

SOME SNAFFLES

6

'Of every twenty bits I make nineteen are for men's heads and one for the horse's'

I have mentioned in a previous chapter that the principal division in the snaffle group comes between the mullen mouth (half-moon) variety and the jointed types.

The mullen mouth bits, softer in their action than the jointed ones, are fewer in number, and variation occurs only in the material from which the mouthpiece is made and in the construction of the bit rings. The mildest form has a flexible indiarubber mouth with a chain through the centre for the sake of safety (Fig. 28). It is useful for youngsters, particularly racehorses, who may be frightened of going on to the bit and may be very light

28. *Rubber snaffle.*

29. *Eggbutt snaffle.*

mouthed. Conversely, it is recommended for pullers, the idea being that as the horse pulls against pain, it is reasonable to suppose that if the source of the pain is removed and something much softer substituted the animal will have nothing to pull against.

If you are only half convinced by this argument, a slightly stronger mouthpiece is available in vulcanite and an even stronger one in plain metal.

A further type of mullen mouthpiece of thick rolled leather, usually a soft rawhide, is occasionally made with the object of encouraging the horse to mouth his bit. I have made these bits but never used one; nor, to be honest, have I ever had any great success with the other mullen mouthpieces. Apart from racing, I find that horses tend to hang on them, but this may be the fault of my hands and not of the bit.

The rings in any type of snaffle, where the bit rings are loose as opposed to being fixed like an eggbutt, are either rounded, when they are known as 'wire' rings, or flat in shape. The former are always preferable for the reason that they require a smaller hole in the mouthpiece through which to pass and there is consequently less danger of pinching the lips.

A second division in the snaffle group lies between bits with loose rings, and those with fixed rings like the eggbutt (Fig. 29), the dee cheek (Fig. 30), and the normal cheek snaffles (Fig. 31).

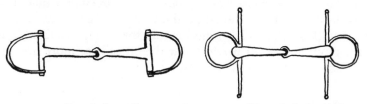

30. Dee cheek snaffle.   *31. Normal cheek snaffle.*

The dee cheek and the eggbutt developed, in that order, from the cheek snaffle. In Latchford's time (his book *The Loriner* was published in 1883) all forms of snaffle mouthpieces were fitted with cheeks, as in Fig. 31. With the exception of the bit (Fig. 32) which I term an Australian loose ring cheek snaffle (and it was called this a hundred years ago) and which is now better known as a Fulmer snaffle, there are not many of them in use today, the eggbutt having replaced them in the popularity poll.

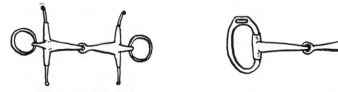

32. Australian loose ring cheek snaffle.   *33. Eggbutt snaffle with slot in ring.*

Eggbutt snaffles (or dee cheeks or plain cheeks) have certain advantages, the first being that they cannot be slid through the mouth to evade the action. Secondly, they minimise the chances of pinching the lips. With this form of ring they are, however, fixed in the mouth with little play in the mouthpiece. Contrariwise, the mouthpiece fitted with loose rings affords considerable play, allowing the horse to mouth the bit and make saliva with a subsequent relaxing of the jaw. While normally the eggbutt suits many horses, it would not be a wise choice for a dry-mouthed animal who might be stiff in his jaw. From a purely personal viewpoint, I prefer a loose ring snaffle, and providing a wire ring is used and the hole through which it passes is not worn, there is little danger of pinching. As far as sliding through the mouth goes, a normal 3½-in. diameter ring will make this habit difficult. Some trainers, to avoid sliding and to keep the horse straight, use exceptionally large rings up to as much as 4½ in.

If, however, I wanted an eggbutt bit, appreciating that it was fixed in the mouth, I should go the whole hog and have a slot in the ring (Fig. 33), which would ensure that it (*a*) was fixed in the right position and (*b*) would allow the bit to bear more upon the bars than the corners of the lips.

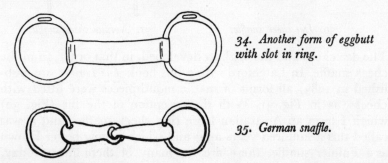

34. Another form of eggbutt with slot in ring.

35. German snaffle.

Prior to the last war a very useful form of eggbutt snaffle with a slot in the ring and a broad, flat, curved metal mouthpiece was in vogue (Fig. 34). The slots in the rings ensured that the mouthpiece always lay flat over the tongue and across the bars. The width of the mouthpiece allowed a widely distributed surface pressure on the bars and the consequent downward action permitted a degree of flexion unobtainable in ordinary snaffles. This bit was produced by Lieut.-Col. F. E. Gibson for a client of his and was marketed under the name of the Distas snaffle, this being the name of his firm at that time. I believe it was also called the Weedon snaffle at one stage and was used there. Unfortunately, the bit is no longer made and, unless it should suddenly come into fashion, it is unlikely that it will be seen again.

In a previous chapter I mentioned the importance of a good broad mouthpiece and today, even in the racing world, ever obsessed with the problem of weight, where the thinnest of mouthpieces were once to be found, the tendency now is for them to be fairly thick and comfortable.

A good example of this trend is demonstrated by the growing popularity of the German snaffle (Fig. 35), which has a hollow mouthpiece and is ideal for the young horse. The mouthpiece is also reproduced with an eggbutt ring (Fig. 36) and also in the Australian loose ring snaffle (or Fulmer if you would prefer). This latter bit, much used in the training of the young horse, obviates my objection to the usually fixed nature of this type of bit by having its rings set on independently of the cheek, thereby allowing considerable mouthing of the bit. As in all cheek snaffles, the cheeks facilitate the lateral movement of the head by being pressed up against one or other side of the face—a great help with a green youngster.

36. German snaffle with eggbutt ring.   *37. 'Dick Christian' snaffle.*

It is customary with this snaffle to secure the top of the cheeks to the cheekpiece of the bridle by means of a short connecting strap, known as a 'cheek retainer'. This has the advantage of keeping the cheek in an upright position, but to a certain extent nullifies the otherwise admirable loose ring by reducing the extent of the 'mouthing' movement that was previously possible. Nevertheless this bit by whatever name it is called (as Mr Hall of Fulmer has done more than anyone else to bring it to the attention of the riding public, I think it can be fairly renamed after his establishment) is an exceedingly useful one.

Quite a number of snaffles depart from the usual central joint and are made with either a link in the centre as in the Dick Christian (Fig. 37) or with a spatula as in the French bradoon (Fig. 38). By the insertion of this link the nutcracker action is lessened and the link or spatula which rests on the tongue gives greater comfort. Such a construction also minimises the danger of the tongue being pinched in the joint. The former is named after the great hunting character of the last century, Dick Christian, and a version of this bit appears in Latchford's book under this name.

Today it is made with a broad aluminium mouthpiece with the connecting link of steel, and is a good bit for tender-mouthed youngsters.

The French bradoon is either available as a bradoon for use in a double bridle, and as such was used by the famous Cadre Noir, or with larger rings as a snaffle. Mr Fred Rimell, the trainer, finds them helpful, I believe, particularly with horses who are fussy about their mouths.

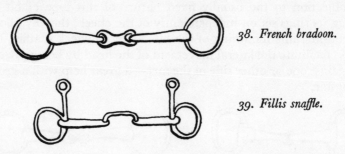

38. French bradoon.

39. Fillis snaffle.

Another bit, of a somewhat similar type, is the Fillis snaffle (Fig. 39), called after James Fillis and made popular some years ago by Mrs Dorothy Popoff. At her instigation a considerable number of these bits were produced and proved very successful in many spheres. In this instance the bit is suspended in the mouth (as opposed to resting on it) and is jointed at either side of the central port, thus reducing the squeezing action. This port allows room for the tongue; a fact that is not always generally realised or catered for—i.e. that in some animals the tongue is almost too big for the mouth and can accordingly become an obstacle to comfortable bitting. With the tongue having sufficient room to lie normally, however, many of the difficulties encountered with this type of animal disappear. Mrs Popoff particularly recommended this bit for animals who tended to get 'over' the bit (discomfort of the tongue contributing to this evasion), with the resultant stiffness of the back which this produced. (See explanation 'above the bit' in Chapter 13.) Unfortunately this most useful bit has largely disappeared, not because of the lack of public demand, even though its sale was never great, but because the difficulties of construction could be overcome only by having it hand-forged. As this is virtually a lost art, production of the bit at the present time has ceased. It is possible, however, that the bit may in the future be made by a casting process and so perhaps make a reappearance on the market.

Prior to the last war, other patterns were produced incorporating the same cheek and suspended action as the Fillis and with a mouthpiece similar to the French bradoon. A bit of this type known as the Ostrich was used for racing and there were others of a similar construction used as a bradoon in conjunction with a curb bit. The suspended nature of the bit combined with the central spatula was a most comfortable one and it is a pity that they are now difficult to obtain.

'STRONG' BITS

There is then the category of snaffle bits which I term 'strong', not always because they are severe in their action but because their employment is generally confined to strong-mouthed animals.

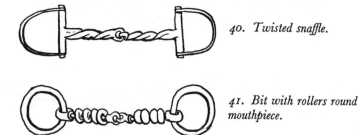

40. Twisted snaffle.

41. Bit with rollers round mouthpiece.

First, of course, is the common twisted snaffle (Fig. 40), made with either loose rings or a dee or eggbutt fitting; they are obvious enough to require no explanation. Secondly, there are those bits with rollers set either round the mouthpiece (Fig. 41) or across it like the Magenis (Fig. 42). Snaffles are not the only types of bit among which rollers round the mouth are to be found; they also occur among various members of the Pelham family and could conceivably be incorporated in a curb bit. They are not nearly so fierce as they perhaps look at first sight, and their purpose is to distract the horse by encouraging him to mouth his bit, and so to make it difficult for him to seize hold of it and tear away like an express train. The addition of rollers to the mouthpiece does, therefore, give us far greater control without, I believe, the infliction of severe pain.

The Magenis (this is the correct name, although it has many

others derived from those experts who have found it useful) has its rollers set across the mouth within the mouthpiece itself, the latter often being squared off at the edges. This is a stronger bit, but again is designed to give the rider greater control over a powerful horse and in particular over one who crosses or sets his jaw against the bit, the rollers being set in this fashion making it difficult for the animal to achieve this type of evasion. It is used frequently and with success on show jumpers and is a favourite with Colonel Talbot-Ponsonby.

I remember discussing this bit with a foreign competitor, whose name I cannot remember, at one of the London shows. He maintained that its greatest value was realised when the rider introduced a *gentle* sawing action by running the rollers to and fro

42. 'Magenis' snaffle.

43. 'Scorrier' or 'Cornish' snaffle.

44. 'Y mouth' or 'W mouth' snaffle.

45. Spring Mouth snaffle.

across the mouth. A lowering of the head was thus induced and this, combined with the action of the leg, made collection of the horse and the 'giving' of the lower jaw quickly attainable. I am quite sure he was right and one day if I get that sort of horse (and if my hands improve) I shall try it.

The Scorrier (Fig. 43), sometimes called the 'Cornish' snaffle, is yet another 'strong' bit. It varies from the usual run of riding snaffles by having four rings instead of two, such an arrangement being known as Wilson rings. The two inside rings are fixed in slots within the mouthpiece itself (the inside or bearing surface of the mouthpiece is grooved or serrated); these rings are then attached to the cheekpieces of the bridle while the outside rings are for the rein alone. The result of using the four rings in this way is to give a greater, direct effect to the rein, the inside rings on the cheeks of the bridle not giving the slight upward restraint that mitigates the backward pull of the rein when both cheek and rein are fastened to one ring. When pressure is applied to the bit by means of the rein, the inside rings produce an inward squeezing action on the sides of the jaw, and this, together with the more powerful action of the rein and the serrated edge of the bit, can be fairly described as a strong restraining force.

The 'Y mouth' or 'W mouth' snaffle, with two mouthpieces (Fig. 44) set so that the joints are one on either side, obtains its name from the shape it takes on when pressure is applied on the rein. This I regard as an unpleasant bit and one in which considerable pinching of the lips and probably the tongue, too, is possible. I cannot really think that it is a very sensible bit.

Last of the more common bits in this category is the Spring Mouth (Fig. 45) or 'butterfly' bit, which is not really a bit but an attachment. It is clipped on to the rings of a snaffle to give a fairly strong additional action in the mouth and, although with good hands and used only occasionally, it may be effective on a head-strong subject, I do not like to see it inflicted on keen jumping ponies by children who are over-horsed.

SNAFFLE BRIDLES

There remain three snaffle bridles as opposed to bits where the combination is such that their action is a little outside that of their family group. The three are the Rockwell, the Norton Perfection (the horse Citation wore a bridle of this type and it is sometimes so named) and a near relative of the Rockwell, the Newmarket. Incidentally I have never seen the last named ever used in Newmarket, though it may have acquired its name by being confused with the Rockwell. I have a feeling that this was also known as the Weedon bridle, which is probably a more appropriate name.

The first two are almost exclusive to racing. The Rockwell (Fig. 46) is the milder of the two and consists of an ordinary fairly thick mouthpiece, round which the lower loop of a metal figure of eight link is permanently attached; the top loops then have an adjustable elastic nosepiece attached to them, which in turn is supported by a strap running up the nose through a central slot on the browband and fastening to the head of the bridle. By combining pressure on the nose with the action of the snaffle, the head is lowered, giving greater control on a pulling horse. In addition, there is the important psychological restraint imposed by the divided central strap running up the face. Anything of this nature dissuades a horse from poking his nose and getting his head into a high and uncontrollable position. The nosepiece also tends to lift the bit in the mouth making it a little more difficult for the horse to get his tongue over it (a habit discussed in Chapter 12) should he be addicted to this evasion.

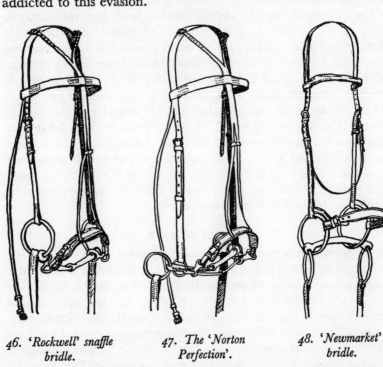

46. 'Rockwell' snaffle bridle.

47. The 'Norton Perfection'.

48. 'Newmarket' bridle.

The Norton Perfection (Fig. 47) employs, like the Scorrier, four rings with the reins on the outside ones, but two mouthpieces, the inside one, which has metal loops to which the nosepiece is attached, being particularly thin and sharp. It produces a squeezing action on the jaw similar to the Scorrier and otherwise operates in much the same way, if not more severely than the Rockwell. It should stop practically anything on four legs!

The Newmarket bridle (Fig. 48), now much neglected, is not a racing requisite but rather an extremely good training bridle for a young horse. Its action can be clearly seen from the illustration and one would use it on a young horse to obtain a lowered position of the head through the medium of the nose before starting with a double bridle. Those who still dislike the dropped noseband as a training aid might well adopt this bridle and so delay putting their young horses into a double one. As far as I can remember I have made only two Newmarket bridles in seven years, but I still think it might play a reasonable part in the training curriculum.

The snaffle family is a very large one and I have, therefore, only mentioned those either in common use or of special interest. I realise that there are many I have omitted, but, generally, they will be found to be variants of the better known ones or ones accentuating a particular characteristic of the parent.

Snaffle bits are measured between the rings when laid flat. The following measurements are a rough guide (for jointed snaffles) as to the sizes to which they are applicable.

6 in.–5¾ in.	Usual hunter size.
5½ in.–5¼ in.	Medium size (14·2–15 h.h.).
5 in.–4¾ in.	Pony sizes.

A mullen mouthpiece is again measured between the rings, the sizes being:

5½ in.	Full hunter.
5¼ in.	Blood horses.
5 in.	Medium size (14·2–15 h.h.).
4¾ in. and 4½ in.	Pony sizes.

THE DOUBLE BRIDLE

7

*'There are three kinds of fool: the fool, the damn
fool and the fool that hunts in a snaffle' (There is
one more—the fool that believes this.—Author)*

The double bridle consists of a bradoon or snaffle bit and a curb
bit. In former days when the accent in bitting was on the curb bit,
there was an impressive array of shapes and types available and
even now one can savour the names they bore: 'Harry Highover',
'Melton', 'Bentinck', 'Thurlow' and so on. Today with the accent

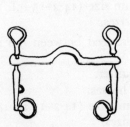

49. *Slide cheek 'Weymouth'
bit.*

50. *Fixed cheek
'Weymouth' bit.*

shifting as the snaffle becomes more widely appreciated, the
variety is smaller and for practical purposes we can divide the
group into three—the ordinary Weymouth bit with a slide cheek,
the Weymouth with the fixed cheek, and the Banbury.

The slide cheek Weymouth (Fig. 49) is the most common and is
so called because the cheek does slide to a very limited extent in
the mouthpiece. The fixed cheek (Fig. 50), on the other hand,
without such movement in the mouthpiece, is becoming more
prevalent and is, in fact, now compulsory for Three Day Event
dressage tests. Its action is more direct than that of the slide cheek
and it allows a little less leverage because of the absence of movement between cheek and mouthpiece. The mouthpiece is, of

course, fixed in the mouth, which is not the case with the slide cheek type, but this is not of importance by the time one's horse is sufficiently advanced to perform Three Day Event tests. Usually in the English type the bit is used with a loose-ring bradoon, but in the German type of dressage bit and bradoon, the latter is usually an eggbutt. The dressage bit (Fig. 51) has an exceptionally broad mouthpiece, which is admirable, and the port is sometimes slightly offset forward. The mouthpiece of the bradoon is likewise broad and flattish.

As a personal preference I like the bradoon to be 'sloppy' in the mouth and therefore with loose rings, an eggbutt in conjunction

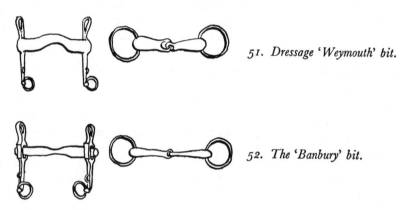

51. Dressage 'Weymouth' bit.

52. The 'Banbury' bit.

with a fixed cheek bit being rather too rigid for my liking. My previous remarks regarding the width of mouthpieces distributing the weight over a greater area are particularly well illustrated in this type of bit. I have loosely termed it 'German' type because it is used in that country, but strangely enough I recently found an illustration of just such a bit in an English manufacturer's catalogue published at the turn of the century. Perhaps after all there is some truth in the saying that fashion has a habit of repeating itself.

In both types of bit, the severity depends upon the length of cheek which allows greater or lesser leverage according to its length. It should be noted, however, that there are variations (not so common in modern bit production) between the length of the cheek above the mouthpiece and the length below it, as well as differences in its total length. A cheek in which there is a long length above the mouthpiece will give not only greater leverage but greater poll pressure than a short one.

In normal production types the total length of the cheek is the same as the width of the mouthpiece—i.e. a 5½-in. mouthpiece with a 5½-in. cheek with the length above the cheek being between 1½ in. and 1¾ in. Longer or shorter cheeks are, however, available even to the extreme of the aptly named 'Tom Thumb' cheek. This is a very short cheek not exceeding 3½ in. in its overall length and is consequently extremely mild in its action. The depth of the port, as I have explained previously, by allowing more or less room for the tongue, controls the amount of pressure imposed upon the bars. In cases where it is thought advisable to put little or no pressure on the bars, a mullen mouthpiece to give greater bearing on the tongue can be obtained in either a fixed or slide cheek bit.

The principles regarding the length of cheek are equally applicable to the Banbury bit (Fig. 52), but here the mouthpiece is a round bar tapered in the centre to allow a little room for the tongue. The mouthpiece is fitted into slots in the cheek, enabling it both to revolve and move up and down in the mouth. The object is to allow the animal to mouth the bit and also to prevent him catching hold of it. I have used it only once, on a particularly hard-mouthed Indian country-bred, and it certainly gave me as much control as anything would on an animal of that description. As they are loose, the cheeks can, of course, be made to work independently of each other, which may prove useful on the type of animal who is ridden in this bit. In spite of the tapering of the mouthpiece, the pressure is bound to be greater on the tongue than on the bars.

With the disappearance of hand-forging and the saddler's almost complete reliance upon cast metal bits, individual preferences for ports or mouthpieces of a particular and exact shape outside the scope of the normal production moulds are unlikely to be satisfied, and I think it is highly improbable (and possibly unnecessary) that there will be any increase in the shapes and types that are at present available. Mouthpieces are at present stocked in ¼-in. sizes from 4¼ in. to 5½ in. and correspond to the size of animal as shown in the table at the end of Chapter 6, which refers to mullen mouth bits.

8 THE PELHAM

'Compromises are rarely satisfactory to either side'

No group of bits seems to have received so much attention from the pundits as this one, and as a result the Pelham appears in an almost confusing welter of differing shapes, all purporting to improve its basic action. None of them, of course, surmounting the fact that it is still trying to do two jobs with one mouthpiece. Nevertheless its continued popularity shows that it does in one or other of its shapes fulfil a need.

Apart from the normal mullen mouthpiece made either in metal, vulcanite or flexible rubber (Fig. 53), the shape of mouthpiece can vary considerably.

The most efficient shape to my mind is found in the Arch Mouth Pelham (Fig. 54), where the mouthpiece has an upward curve allowing ample room for the tongue and permitting the bit to lie across the bars of the mouth as opposed to lying on the tongue as it does with the mullen mouthpiece.

The Hartwell Pelham (Fig. 55) is also constructed with this object in view, but has a normal ported mouthpiece, which in the Pelham bit I do not regard as quite so efficient as the arched mouth.

The Jointed Pelham (Fig. 56), by reason of its construction, adds the familiar nutcracker action to its repertoire and, by so doing, seems to me to be trying to do too much and failing to achieve one definite action. In the use of this bit the curb chain must be passed through the top rein loop of the bit if it is going to produce any form of pressure. Without this adjustment, the curb chain will fall away from the groove when the mouthpiece assumes a 'V'-shape in the mouth in response to pressure on the snaffle rein. This is also true to a lesser degree with a flexible rubber mouthpiece. I class this bit under a group headed 'Hotchpotch', because it tries to do too much and does nothing well.

The Hanoverian mouthpiece (Fig. 57), while being fairly 'strong', has a certain amount of logic behind it and is much in demand for children's ponies and to a lesser extent for polo. The mouthpiece is jointed as before, but on either side of the central port. The rollers on the mouthpiece act in exactly the same way as rollers on a snaffle, but because of the port bear rather more on to the bars. Even with the lesser degree of nutcracker effect made possible by the two joints in the mouthpiece, I would still put the curb chain through the top ring. Occasionally, particularly in older bits of this type, the port may be so high as to bear upon the roof of the mouth and this makes an already strong bit into a severe one.

One of the disadvantages of the Pelham is that it does tend to chafe the lips and just above the corners of the mouth.

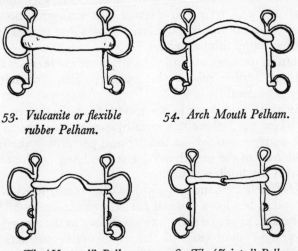

*53. Vulcanite or flexible
rubber Pelham.*

54. Arch Mouth Pelham.

55. The 'Hartwell' Pelham.

56. The 'Jointed' Pelham.

The Scamperdale (Fig. 58), popularised by Mr Sam Marsh, very sensibly overcomes this by having the mouthpiece turned back at each end to bring the cheekpiece an inch or so farther back and away from the area where chafing occurs. Otherwise it does not alter the action in any definite sense, although obviously this must be improved if the horse is comfortable.

The S.M. Pelham (Fig. 59), now out of fashion and almost out of production too, is in fact of American origin and was introduced to this country by Messrs Distas in the 1930's. The cheeks, which move independently in a restricted arc (restricted because of the small stud set on the mouthpiece, which also has an arc of movement of the same degree), are combined with a broad flat mouth-piece, ported to allow room for the tongue and giving again the desirable wide coverage over the bars. I am, as readers will have gathered, not a devotee of Pelhams, but this particular one, in spite of having the defects common to its family, does appear to have several points in its favour.

The Rugby Pelham (Fig. 60), made either with a plain mouth or with the addition of a port and rollers, lies within the province of

57. *The 'Hanoverian' mouthpiece.*

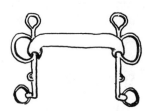

58. *The 'Scamperdale'.*

59. *The S.M. Pelham.*

60. *The 'Rugby' Pelham.*

the polo man. The cheek is a fixed one and the setting of the snaffle ring on an independent link makes it not unlike a curb bit, allowing stronger and more clearly defined curb and poll pressure.

A Pelham, which has all the characteristics of a curb bit and is, therefore, not strictly a Pelham but rather a curb bit used independently of a bradoon, is the Globe cheek Pelham (Fig. 61)—sometimes known, incorrectly, as a Hunloke Pelham. It is used in children's pony classes and occasionally arouses the wrath of those doubtless sincere people who become so obsessed with an anti-cruelty complex as to see cruelty in innocent things.

The action of the Globe cheek is the same as that of any curb bit—i.e. a downward and inward one produced by pressure on the bars, poll and curb groove. Normally the cheek is so short that there is little danger of the animal becoming overbent, although the possibility of this happening cannot be eliminated, particularly if the pony's early training has been incorrectly carried out. As a general rule, when a very small child is concerned, I can see nothing very wrong in its use and certainly no cruelty.

Occasionally one will see a similar bit appearing in hack classes (see Fig. 62, Show Hack bit) and I cannot remember anyone criticising the late R. E. Pritchard for having one.

The Banbury mouthpiece incorporated in a Pelham (Fig. 63) has the same objective as when used in the form of a curb bit and was discussed in the previous chapter.

61. 'Globe' cheek Pelham.

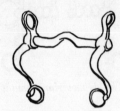

62. Show Hack bit.

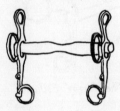

63. The 'Banbury' mouthpiece.

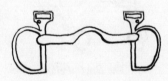

64. The 'Kimblewick'.

An important member of the Pelham group is the Kimblewick (Fig. 64). It was an adaptation of a Spanish jumping bit produced by Lieut.-Col. F. E. Gibson for Phil Oliver and so named by him after the village where Mr Oliver lived. It became extremely popular as a jumping bit, and various slight variations were produced, or even outright copies, and called by such names as 'Kimberwick'. Its action, the combination of snaffle and curb bit, is purely Pelham, but the squared eye as opposed to the usual rounded one allows considerably more downward pressure on the poll. It achieves its object of lowering the head to the position best calculated to give control, by allowing the rein to slip slightly down the cheek when the hand is lowered, thus causing immediate and direct poll and curb pressure combined with a downward action of the mouthpiece on the bars. It is important to remember that a low position of the hands is essential if the full effect is to be achieved.

Over employed, the Kimblewick tends to make a horse hang on the bit and the hands, and I would reserve it as an extremely effective 'change' bit. In the case of a particularly exuberant thoroughbred horse of my own, I found it very successful for hunting and jumping, but otherwise always rode him in a plain snaffle.

This bit too has its critics and I know of two first-rate horsemen and horsemasters, whom I otherwise admire and with whom I am usually in agreement, who nevertheless condemn it as being unduly severe, and who even go so far as to suggest that it is capable of breaking a jaw. This, I feel, with the greatest respect, is nonsense

65. Angle-cheek Pelham.

66. Swales '3 in 1' Pelham.

and a complete impossibility in a bit of this design. In bad hands it will bruise the lips, but then so will anything else if the rider is that bad. For children, providing they desist from yanking their ponies all over the place, it is a sensible bit for a strong pony and far better than the Pelham fitted with roundings (see Chapter 4).

Two more of the Pelham group are the Army pattern Angle-cheek Pelham (Fig. 65) and Swales '3 in 1' (Fig. 66). The former can be used with either the serrated side of the mouthpiece against the mouth, or with the reverse side, which is smooth. It was designed to suit as wide a variety of mouths as might be found in a cavalry troop, or even a regiment, by changing the mouthpiece and the position of the reins in the cheek slots. As such I suppose it was a clever and workable compromise; otherwise it has nothing to recommend it over and above the usual run of Pelhams.

The Swales bit is a severe one with the squeezing action of the inside rings on the fixed mouthpiece making it uncomfortable. I don't believe that any horse is better controlled by imposing discomfort on him and, even though some horses may go in it, I still regard it as one of those bits without which we and the horse would be better off.

These then are some of the better known types which form the Pelham family; that there are many others I am well aware, but in the main they have either gone out of fashion or production or both and are unlikely to appear again; and, with the passage of time and the acquisition of greater knowledge, it may well be that some of these more common ones will disappear too.

9 | THE GAG

'And be ye lifted up . . .'

The group of gag bits can be divided into two sections—those that are used on their own and those used in a double bridle where they give a greater upward action than a normal bradoon.

67. *Gag with rollers round the mouth.*

68. *'Cheltenham' with eggbutt cheek.*

69. *Gag with 'Duncan' cheek.*

70a. *A 'hack overcheck'.*

In the former category the mouthpiece is usually jointed and smooth or it can be fitted with rollers round the mouth (Fig. 67). This latter, while being an old pattern, has become known as Colonel Rodzianko's gag; the object of the rollers is, of course, as previously explained.

Whether there is an advantage in having an eggbutt cheek on a gag as in the Cheltenham (Fig. 68) is problematical, but some people claim that it drops more quickly when the gag rein is released.

Where a gag is used as a bradoon in the double bridle, the ring must obviously be smaller or can disappear altogether and be replaced with a Duncan check (Fig. 69). There is also a very sharp twisted gag with rings so small that only a cord can pass through the holes in the ring. It is termed a 'hack overcheck' (Fig. 70a) and is a salutary method of raising the head to the correct position. While it might be of assistance to an experienced nagsman, it could be very dangerous in other hands.

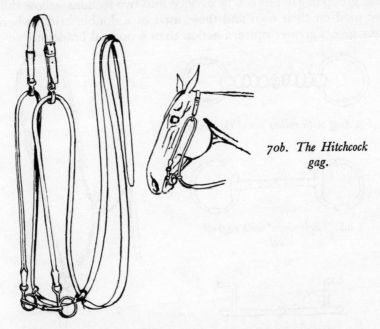

70b. The Hitchcock gag.

In days now long past, gag rings were fixed to Pelham bits to incorporate a gag action in that bit. I remember seeing them on polo ponies and presumably they worked even though such a combination would have seemed to me illogical. A gag used in polo and possessed of a considerable 'winding up' action is that produced by Hitchcock, the American expert after whom it was named. The illustration (Fig. 70b) shows the extent of its elevatory power and gives some idea of the speed with which this can be obtained.

While I have emphasised the gag as a means of head raising, which is its basic function, it is also frequently used in conjunction with a standing martingale as a method of control on very strong, impetuous animals. In this case the ability to raise the head is nullified by the martingale and it becomes merely a strong agent of control, fixing the head by the interplay of the two contradictory forces. Many show jumpers thus bitted already carry their heads so high that a gag on its own would merely make matters worse, if that were possible. The gag, therefore, used in this way against the pull of a tight martingale becomes a means of checking the horse through the sharp upward action against a mouth already fixed in its position and incapable of further elevation. It is not, therefore, surprising that these horses are almost invariably stiff in the poll, neck and back and frequently fail in their efforts to clear big spread fences.

If one has a horse of this type, I have no doubt that this may be an effective and possibly the only way of obtaining control, unless one is prepared to embark on a lengthy process of reschooling which would be the real, if to some people impractical, solution. This procedure still remains, however, opposed to the logical processes of bitting in its disregard for the principle of the employment of the whole horse with the bit as the extension of that employment.

10 | THE BITLESS BRIDLE
'Simplicity is the keynote'

This is a group of bridles used only infrequently, but which do have advantages in certain instances. A bitless bridle need not necessarily be an elaborate affair and quite an effective one can

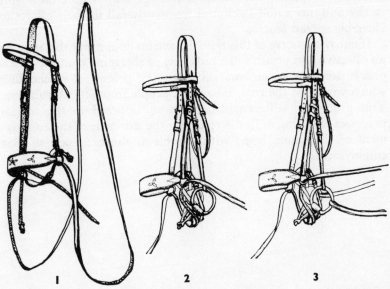

71. The 'Scawbrig' bridle, showing the three methods of use in the training of the horse.

be made with a stout noseband and judiciously placed rings. In fact, with a little thought it is quite easy to produce a very workable one which can be used with or without a bit.

A product of such thought and a refinement on the basic noseband is the Scawbrig bridle (Fig. 71). It is not original in design and many other forms of 'control nosebands', as they are sometimes called, preceded it, but it does illustrate the simpler type of bitless bridle and also reveals the potential of such bridles.

Briefly, it consists of a bridle head and cheeks with a broad nosepiece, a backstrap to hold the nosepiece in place, and a rein which is passed through the two rings at either side of the nosepiece, being joined in the centre by a padded curb piece. In this, its simplest form (Fig. 71 (1)) control is obtained by pressure on the nose and curb groove and by slight poll pressure. If, however, a broader view is taken, the addition of a sliphead can make the bridle into a very useful training device particularly for jumping. In the first stages the horse learns to jump when guided entirely by pressure on the nose, etc., and as there is no bit, his confidence is not damaged by his receiving a jab in the mouth, and so with the absence of pain his training proceeds calmly.

72. *The 'W.S. Bitless Pelham'.*

Later on (Fig. 71 (2)) the sliphead is added and a bit suspended in his mouth without the attachment of a rein. During this period, while still ensuring that his mouth is not touched, he is becoming accustomed to the feel of the bit without it being associated with any pain or discomfort.

The final method (3) entails the addition of a rein to the bit and its increased use, while still having the restraint of the bridle on nose and curb.

As a training bridle it has in fact proved a most successful device in which to teach a horse to jump, as well as the inexperienced rider. It originated some years ago at the home of the Robinette family in Lincolnshire and has been extensively used ever since.

'Blairs' pattern (see Fig. 13) is more restricted in its scope, but is a true bitless bridle. The length of cheek produces sufficient pressure on the nose to restrain any horse who is not mentally afflicted, but it is important to have the nose and curb pieces well padded to avoid chafing. Lateral movement of the head, comparatively easily obtained with the Scawbrig, entails with Blair's pattern an exaggerated opening of the hand before a positive result is obtained.

The 'W.S. Bitless Pelham' (Fig. 72), sometimes known as the Distas bridle (W.S. are the initials of William Stone, who is connected with bit-making in the Midlands and who has been instrumental in producing many of the more uncommon demands made upon him by saddlers) is another true 'bitless' bridle and shorter in the cheeks, which are also movable and not fixed. It is designed for use with two reins, the lower one operating the curb chain so that pressure can be applied to either nose or curb groove with some degree of independence.

CURB CHAINS AND OTHER BIT ACCESSORIES

11

'For the sake of a nail the shoe was lost, for the sake of . . .'

Curb chains or curbs are made either of a series of linked metal rings or of leather or elastic. In the first case the links may be single ones or double to form a kind of mesh (Fig. 73). In either case there is often a variation in the width and, on the principle of distributing pressure over as large an area as possible, I prefer a broad-linked chain to a narrow one, which might be too cutting in its action.

73–77. *Curb chains. From top to bottom: links forming a mesh; leather curb; elastic curb; rubber curb guard; 'Jodhphor' polo curb.*

A leather curb (Fig. 74), often termed 'humane', is a good one and providing it is kept soft and is properly adjusted will no cause chafing.

The elastic curb (Fig. 75) is as effective as any and particularly so on horses who may resent the curb action, and just as much result can be obtained from this type as by using the more usual metal one.

Should a metal curb cause soreness, a rubber curb guard (shown in Fig. 76), through which the chain is slipped, is a simple remedy.

The Jodhphor polo curb (Fig. 77) is a stronger device, the oval-shape fitting between the jaw bones and exerting considerable pressure.

Curb hooks sometimes cause discomfort and chafing and if a horse is invariably found to be sore because of them, the Circle pattern curb hook (Fig. 78) will be found to be a good antidote. The hook is so shaped as to lie flat and, therefore, cannot chafe.

78. Circle pattern curb hook.

A lip strap is an essential addition to a bit having a curb chain and will prevent the curb rising out of the curb groove; the rounded leather variety looks neater but a flat leather one will last longer.

In cases where a snaffle bit or a Pelham is pinching or chafing the lips, a pair of thin rubber cheek guards are the ideal preventive. The rubber is sufficiently flexible to be pulled over a 4-in. bit ring without tearing. Circles of leather fastened round the mouthpiece with a lace are not nearly so satisfactory, as the lace itself can chafe and the leather becomes hard in use.

All these items are small enough in themselves, but as our object is to make sure that no unnecessary discomfort is caused in the process of bitting the horse, it is essential that we should realise their value.

12 | COMMON EVASIONS AND SOME REMEDIES

'No horse was born a rogue but man made him so'

The horse can produce an alarming number of evasions to the various indications of the bit, many being caused by incorrect early training. Some of these can be cured by a course of retraining, but some remain obstinately with us and defy our efforts to cure them. I do not suggest that any of the articles dealt with in this chapter are certain cures, but they can work even if they are not always a hundred per cent successful.

79. *Rubber tongue port.*

80. *The 'Nagbut' snaffle.*

One of the most common evasions is that of getting the tongue over the bit, and so preventing the bit achieving its action and also minimising the extent of our control. Usually this is caused by too large a breaking bit, particularly if it is a jointed one, hanging too low in the mouth during the early stages of training. Such a bit positively encourages the horse to put his tongue over the top. A second cause may be found in a horse getting his tongue pinched or experiencing some form of discomfort on that organ and trying to avoid this by getting his tongue out of the way and over the top. Lastly, his mouth may be sore or damaged and again he tries to remove the pain by clamping the bit underneath his tongue.

Whatever the cause, the resultant habit is a frustrating one and the first thing to realise is that you are unlikely to cure it while the animal has a jointed snaffle in his mouth. A mullen mouthpiece, apart from obviating the risk of pinching his tongue is, if adjusted fairly high in the mouth, more difficult to get a tongue over. If this fails, the addition of a rubber tongue port (Fig. 79), which is easily fastened round a mullen mouthpiece and lies flat on the tongue facing to the rear, will make it even more difficult for him and may dissuade him.

There is also a jointed bit (Fig. 80), the Nagbut snaffle, which has a metal port set in the centre which lies on the tongue and

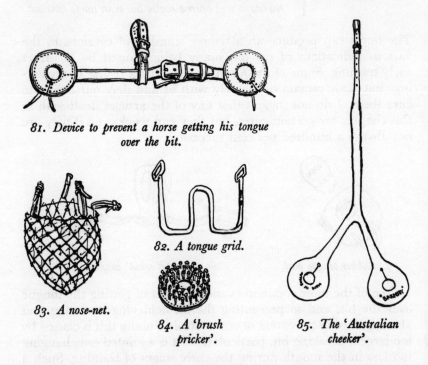

81. *Device to prevent a horse getting his tongue over the bit.*

82. *A tongue grid.*

83. *A nose-net.*

84. *A 'brush pricker'.*

85. *The 'Australian cheeker'.*

achieves the same purpose. Whichever one of these is used, it is important that the horse has no opportunity to slide the bit through the mouth, removing the port from its central position over the tongue.

A device which does in many cases effect a cure is shown in Fig. 81. It consists of the two circular pieces of leather placed round a mullen mouthpiece, the connecting strap being adjusted across the nose and secured by the small central strap to the noseband. This has the effect of raising the bit in the mouth, which is essential, and it also, of course, places pressure on the nose, which is no bad thing in cases of this kind.

A tongue grid (Fig. 82) suspended above the bit will also stop the habit, but is perhaps something of a mouthful.

In racing circles a tongue strap enclosing the tongue and fastened under the lower jaw is occasionally used, but it is at best pretty barbaric and can cause acute pain, even though it ensures that the tongue cannot be moved. It could not be used for anything but short periods and is therefore impracticable outside flat racing. It would, of course, prevent a horse swallowing his tongue—an occasional occurrence—which quickly results in the animal coming to a decided full stop!

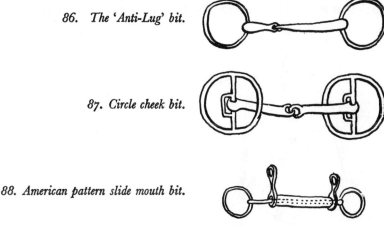

86. The 'Anti-Lug' bit.

87. Circle cheek bit.

88. American pattern slide mouth bit.

Another racing device is the use of the Australian cheeker (Fig. 85), which is made of rubber and lifts the bit in the mouth. The psychological restraint induced by the central portion running up the face is also apparent as in the Rockwell bridle, etc.

In many cases where the habit has not had time to become confirmed, a cure can be brought about by a study of the bit and a change to one employing a different action on the tongue, or better still leaving the tongue alone altogether.

Hard-pulling, runaway horses are also evading the bit and are in fact running away from the pain imposed upon them. A horse that is hard to handle in a plain snaffle may be quite amenable in something a little stronger, but a real tearaway will never be cured of his behaviour by the infliction of more pain on him through increasingly severe bitting. A good rule is to try something very much milder.

If, however, you want to race him or play polo with him and still find him too strong, a very simple device which will nine times out of ten do the trick is a nose-net (Fig. 83). It is put over his nose and fastened fairly tightly to the noseband and will stop the majority of tearaways. It inflicts no pain, but the slight pressure surrounding his tender muzzle, and the very fact that it is there will cause him, as it were, to draw back from it. The effect is largely psychological but it does work. If this and all else fails it were better to shoot the animal before he kills both of you.

Lastly, there are animals who are one-sided of their mouths or stiff in their backs or who, for one reason or another, favour a particular leg so that when racing they hang to one side or another;

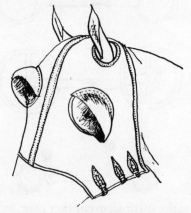

89. Blinkers, with clip fastenings.

and there are also those who have developed a happy knack of running down the length of a fence before screwing over it. In the latter case, the other jockeys will probably effect a cure as far as they are concerned by being so pointed in their remarks that the animal does not appear again until a reformation has been accomplished! Seriously, however, it is important when racing that a horse should run straight and there are a number of articles designed to encourage him to do so. A 'brush pricker' (Fig. 84), on whichever side it is needed, will cause him sufficient surprise and discomfort to change his course. Horses do, however, get used to brush pickers.

The 'Anti-Lug' bit (Fig. 86), with its odd-shaped mouthpiece, will also be of assistance. The short side, which is curved back, is on the opposite side from that to which the horse hangs.

A circle cheek bit (Fig. 87), with its slight squeezing action and large cheekpieces, will again help to keep a horse straight. Another one is (Fig. 88) an American pattern with the rings set on a piece of metal through the mouthpiece itself. In both these cases the bit cannot slide through the mouth, and this is the first object we should try to attain when a horse does show any desire to hang to one side or the other. The Americans with their sharply cornered tracks are far more conscious of steerage than we are, and they have a variety of bits which would rarely be seen, let alone used, in this country.

Lastly blinkers (Fig. 89) are usually worn by horses who 'peek' a bit, don't pay attention, or are just plain doggy. There are numerous patterns, the one with clip fastenings instead of straps being the easiest to get on and off.

The action of nosebands in combating evasions has been discussed in Chapter 5.

13

SCHOOLING MARTINGALES

'They scoff at progress who do not understand it'

In addition to the more common martingales, there are those which simply act as schooling aids or corrective apparatus, and whose aim is to make supple the muscles of the head, neck and back in order to produce a correct positioning and engagement of these parts. As their scope is beyond that of the martingales previously discussed, they being originators of the head carriage and not merely assistants, I have felt they justified a chapter to themselves, and so have chosen three devices to illustrate the potentialities of this group.

Known as the Continental, the Chambon and the De Gogue (Figs. 90, 91, 92), they are all of French origin and with a similar action achieve the same object, which is to induce a lowering and stretching of the head and neck. The result of this, apart from breaking down the resistance in these parts and suppling the relative muscles, is to raise the base of the neck (the balancing agent of the horse) and to exercise the muscles of the back and loins, enabling the back to be rounded, with the consequent engagement of the hocks. They are used frequently in the training of show jumpers, but are equally useful in the schooling of any type of riding horse, particularly those with ewe-necks and consequently hollow backs. Horses in this latter category, particularly, respond extraordinarily well to these schooling devices, which counteract the restriction such a conformation tends to impose upon the free movement of the horse.

A ewe-necked horse or one who 'star gazes' (usually through having its head *pulled* up by the rider's hand rather than *pushed* up by the legs on to a resistant hand) is invariably hollow backed with a resultant cramping of the muscles of the quarters. In this state the horse is 'above the bit' and to a lesser or greater degree—dependent upon the extent to which he is above the bit—the following defects will become apparent.

Action will be retarded and the paces slower; general stiffness, particularly in the hocks, will prevent the stifle and hip joints working to full capacity and the hind toes will probably be dragged; the shoulders will also be cramped, causing the horse to trot and to bend *from* his knees.

As the shoulder muscles remain undeveloped, the saddle will have a tendency to move forward, bringing the girth right under the elbows, probably causing girth galls (no saddle can be constructed to overcome this fault).

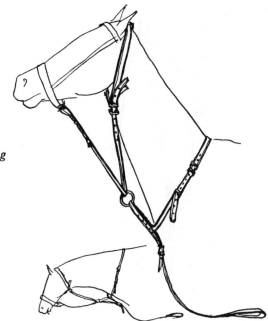

90. 'Continental' schooling martingale.

Similarly, the muscles of back and loin will remain stiff and undeveloped, becoming painful when subjected to the rider's weight and causing the horse to flinch or even to crouch when mounted, and an animal so cramped and stiff will be quite unable to round his back and jump correctly, if indeed he will jump at all.

When the condition becomes as advanced as the one I have described, it does not cure itself and in fact gets worse unless corrective treatment is given.

No horse is born supple, with his muscles developed correctly, and to achieve this development must, therefore, be the principal object of schooling. When we have appreciated this fact and are sufficiently expert to produce a horse so developed, we shall find that many of our bitting problems disappear and, as I have said previously, we shall be able to regard the bit as an extension of the indications given by our seat and legs. The bit, in fact, instead of being regarded only as the fundamental means of obtaining a head carriage conducive to maximum control, will be placed in

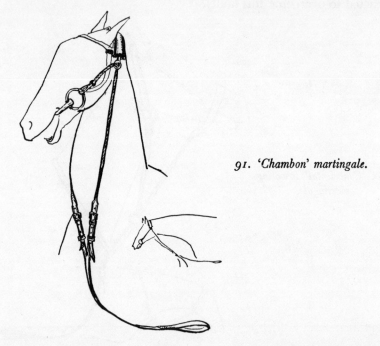

91. 'Chambon' martingale.

its true perspective as part of an harmonious whole. I hope, therefore, that these three martingales will not be dismissed as mere 'gadgets' but will be regarded as useful and logical training aids.

Both the Continental and the Chambon employ pressure on the poll to induce a lowered head carriage. They differ in that the Continental applies pressure between the nose and the poll by means of the strap connecting these two points sliding through a ring on the body of the martingale, while the Chambon is directly connected to the poll from the girth, extending by means of a clip attachment to the rings of the bit. In either case, however, the best results will be gained by working the animal loose in a closed school or some other confined space. A little gentle diplomacy, combined with a reward in the form of some titbit, will get the horse to realise that comfort is in a lowered head carriage. To begin, no pace other than a walk should be attempted and, when the horse lowers his head without resistance at this gait, then a trot can be asked for and work begun to free and develop the muscles of shoulder, back and neck. Gradually the joints of hip, stifle and hock will begin to flex and bend, causing the hocks to be brought well under the body with a consequent improvement in the balance and action of the horse. In neither case should the apparatus be used for more than twenty minutes at a time during the early stages; nor should it be adjusted too tightly. The tension should be increased gradually as the daily schooling proceeds until the head is carried just a little above the level of the knees.

Very occasionally a horse will be met who persists in evading the action by arching his neck, although he may still lower his head well enough. In these cases Benoist-Gironière (author of *The Conquest of the Horse*) recommends that in the case of the Chambon the right-hand cord attached to the bit (which should be a plain mullen mouth rubber snaffle) should be crossed over the face and attached to the nearside bit ring, the nearside attachment being treated in the same way and fastened to the offside ring.

In the case of both these devices, their use is restricted to unmounted work alone (I believe there are one or two people who have attempted ridden work in the Continental, but this is really outside its scope) and it may be that there will be times during the training period, when the horse is ridden, when he will not react as satisfactorily without the restraint of the apparatus to assist him. To overcome this admitted defect, the De Gogue system was produced as an expansion and extension of the Chambon, having far greater possibilities than the latter. The object remains the same, but the means to attain it reveal more advanced thought and allow the horseman to use the device in both unmounted and mounted work.

In its 'independent' position (Fig. 92), the De Gogue is fitted with an additional strap at point A which fastens into the same buckle as the bifurcated strap B and the fastening at point C is attached to this. In this position, unmounted work can be carried out in the same way as with the Chambon, although with this system there is a change in the way in which the head position is controlled. A triangle is formed of the three major resistance points—the poll, mouth and base of the neck. Within the confines of the triangle, the horse can carry his head lowered and with comfort and, after the initial training period required to obtain the lowering of the head, and when sufficient suppleness has been achieved throughout the body, adjustments can then be made to

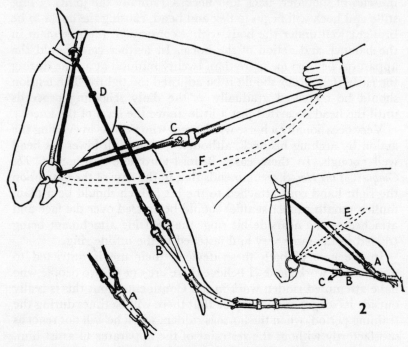

92. 'De Gogue' martingale. Position No. 1 (left) and Position No. 2; independent (right).

bring the nose in and to flex the poll even more. It is not possible to overbend the horse because of a stop (D) placed on the running part of the rein below the small pulley on the poll strap. With the device in this position No. 2, an ordinary rein (indicated by the dotted line E) can then be added for the first stages of mounted work.

The last stage in the system is that shown in position No. 1, where the rein from the hand is directly attached to the roundings at Point C. In this position, the horse can be schooled either on the ground or over fences when the neck will be found to have attained a remarkable degree of elasticity enabling the horse to answer smoothly to the indications of the hand.

It is possible to add a further rein (F) in this position, if it is required, but it is hardly necessary. There is no reason why the De Gogue in this advanced position should not be used for show jumping and cross-country work and in fact M. Rouffe of the Swiss team did use it in both these phases at a recent Three Day Event held at Harewood.

Used as a 'system' of training—and in my opinion the De Gogue justifies this title—the device is logical throughout its sequence, always demanding from the horse the same response by means of similar indications to which he has become accustomed from the beginning of his training.

If the object of training is to produce a horse so supple throughout his body that he is able to obey the directions of the rider without opposition, then certainly the system goes a long way to achieve this end without the danger of encouraging resistances which can arise with other methods.

The De Gogue system is not as yet well known in this country and, until it is, it will tend to arouse suspicion and even ridicule among that section of the horse world (fortunately getting smaller) who instinctively disparage those things which they do not understand.

For instance, I once spent the best part of half an hour explaining the De Gogue to a gentleman who, when I had finished, remarked: 'Yes, of course, nothing new though. Just a standing martingale, really,' and departed muttering about double bridles!! I did, however, try!

Obviously the De Gogue must remain within the province of the more accomplished horseman who can appreciate its value and is therefore capable of obtaining the maximum benefit from it; but, on the other hand, it is very foolish of others to condemn out of hand what is after all a very useful and successful system without carefully studying either its principles or its potential.

I must here acknowledge the debt I owe to Mrs Dorothy Popoff, who first introduced the Continental to me, thereby arousing my interest in this and similar forms of schooling apparatus.

14

SADDLE TREES, CONSTRUCTION AND PANELS

'In the beginning . . .'

The tree (Fig. 93) or framework around which a saddle is built is traditionally made from beechwood. The head and gullet are strengthened with steel plates and there is also a steel reinforcement laid on to the underside of the tree from the head to the cantle. The wood itself is covered in skrim and coated with a black glue-like mixture to make it waterproof.

I say that the tree is traditionally made of beechwood, but many modern trees are now made of laminated wood bonded under pressure and formed in a mould. This laminated process was first introduced some years ago when a crisis occurred in the tree-making industry and beechwood trees were in short supply; and it is certainly an improvement on beechwood, combining greater strength with lightness. An added advantage is, of course, that all the trees are made in one mould and hence all are the same shape, whereas in the older method the beechwood trees, made individually, would not necessarily all be identical.

Other materials are being tried out at the present time, but none so far appears to approach the standard obtained in the partial production line method now employed in the manufacture of the laminated trees. Plastic can be used in tree-making, but would seem to offer no advantages, and some serious defects, notably that it is a difficult material into which to put tacks. Fibreglass has been used and as far as I know still is employed to a limited extent. Recently fibreglass trees have been used successfully in the production of the very light flat-racing saddles, particularly in South Africa, but this, I believe, is the limit of their value.

As far as shapes and sizes of trees are concerned, these cover a wide range and are measured by the length from head to cantle and by the width across the broadest part of the seat. It is noticeable that in post-war years saddles, and consequently trees, have become smaller, rarely now exceeding 18in. in length. Upon the shape of the tree depends the shape of the saddle, and shapes vary from the flat-race tree weighing only a few ounces to the modern dip-seated spring tree.

Trees for normal riding, as opposed to racing, can either be made with a round cantle or a square one. There is no disadvantage or advantage in either.

Cut-back trees—i.e. those cut away at the head—are made to give clearance of the withers when these are particularly pro-

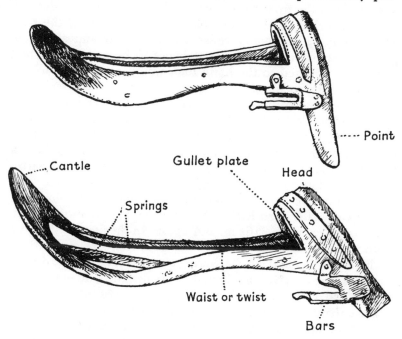

93. Ordinary tree (above) and spring tree (below).

nounced. Such trees are made from a quarter cut-back to a full cut-back; this last is sometimes known as a cow-mouth and is popular in a pet abomination of mine, the American show saddle. This saddle fits closely to the back, has a flat seat designed to put the rider as nearly as possible over the loins of the animal and, having put him there, then has to have enormous flaps extending to within a few inches of the cantle in order that the leg should not lie on the horse itself. An abominable saddle for any purpose, I consider.

In the modern spring tree of correct design (there are badly designed trees), the necessity for a cut-back head is largely obviated by the fact that the head itself is set back at an angle of 45 degrees (see Fig. 93) and thus achieves, although without deliberate intention, the same effect as a cut-back head.

The spring tree itself is discussed in greater detail in the chapter concerned with the evolution of the modern saddle. It is therefore sufficient to say here that the springs consist of two pieces of light steel set from the front to the rear of the tree on the underside, some two inches on the inside of the broadest part of the seat. These springs give greater resilience to the seat and allow the pressure exerted through the seat bones to be more easily and directly transmitted to the horse than would be the case with a tree not having such a seat.

A tree without springs is known as a 'rigid tree' and is found in all types of saddles, including show saddles, race exercise, children's saddles, etc., with the exception of those which I term 'modern' saddles and which are usually marked as 'spring trees' and have a characteristically dipped seat. The main division in saddle trees comes, therefore, between the rigid tree and the spring tree.

Rigid trees are normally obtainable in length sizes from 14 in. (and occasionally even less) to 18 in. and spring trees usually in three sizes—i.e. 15 in., 16½ in. and 17½ in. In the first anything up to 16 in. is suitable for children and from that size onwards for adults, according to their size. Spring trees, because of their dipped shape and the purpose for which they are designed, do not need to be long and 16½ in. will suit all but the largest of riders.

The stirrup bars fitted on to the tree, behind the head and on to the point of the tree, are an integral part of the tree's construction, and on good-quality saddles are always forged; conversely on a cheap saddle using a cheap tree, the bars are cast and their reliability is suspect. The word 'forged' or 'cast' is always stamped on the bar. Bars are normally made in two pieces: the bar itself and a movable catch or 'thumbpiece', as it is called, which is set into the bar. This catch works on the basis that it can be closed when the stirrup leather is in position and will, in theory, open and release the leather if the rider falls. I have never seen anyone ride with the thumbpieces in the closed position, nor would I advise anyone to do so, and I cannot think why this anachronism has survived. It would be far less trouble, far cheaper and far more satisfactory to make a bar in one piece with the end curved upwards as the Australians do. Its origin probably lies in the numerous so-called 'safety bars' much in vogue before and between the two wars. These ingenious devices, which were hinged in various ways to open up and release the stirrup leather when the occasion demanded, have largely disappeared. Occasionally, however, a pattern known as Passmore & Cole bars is asked for and obtained.

Personally, I have always regarded them as anything but safety bars because of their annoying habit of releasing the leather at all kinds of inopportune moments, usually when one least expects or wants them to do so. I also dislike them because of the quite unnecessary bulk they form under the thigh. On modern trees the bars are frequently recessed by being placed on the underside of the tree to avoid causing such bulk. In ninety-nine cases out of a hundred, one avoids being dragged by using a pair of good, large, heavy irons which fall away from the foot.

In the construction of the saddle, the setting up of the seat, using the tree as a foundation, is an all-important operation, and in a good-quality saddle great care and not a little time are expended on this phase. Pre-strained webs are fastened tightly from the head (pommel) of the tree to the cantle to form a foundation, over which is tacked a piece of stretched canvas. 'Bellies' (small pieces of shaped felt and leather) are then placed on the edges of the tree at the broadest part of the seat so that when the seat is eventually made it will not drop away at the edges. Over all this is then put tightly stretched serge stitched down to form the seat shape, in which a small slit is made so that the space between serge and canvas can be lightly stuffed with wool to give the seat resilience and to prevent the tree itself being felt through the leather seat. Finally the pigskin seat is stretched on, and to this are welted in the skirts which cover the bars. For those who appreciate maximum comfort, or for those to whom nature has not been over generous, a piece of sorbo-rubber can be inserted between the pigskin and the serge of the seat.

In a cheap saddle this process of setting the seat can be considerably reduced, a piece of firm jute replacing the canvas and the leather being put on top of that. Such a seat will neither retain its shape nor be comfortable and the saddle's only advantage, if it can be termed that, is in a reduction in the price.

To the tree also are attached the saddle flaps and lastly the panel. The panel is really a cushion, divided by a channel which gives clearance to the horse's backbone, between the horse's back and the tree. If badly made, the panel will not only cause discomfort to the horse but will also hinder the rider in his efforts to sit correctly.

THE PANELS

There are four distinct shapes which the panel can take: full panel (Fig. 94), short panel (Fig. 95), Saumur panel (Fig. 96) and Continental panel (Fig. 97). Individual saddlers may vary slightly in the way they make the last two, and may even call them all by different names from those I have given, but this is not important; basically all shapes will be found to correspond with these four.

These panel shapes evolved in the order I have placed them. The full panel is the oldest and is still in use; properly made with the quilted part kept thin and a slight roll for the knee, it is quite good and the large area of bearing surface it affords to the back is excellent from the horse's viewpoint.

Its disadvantage lies in the fact that, should the quilted part be thick, the rider has little contact with the horse and the wide bearing surface at the waist of the saddle will open his thighs. Early saddles (early and mid-nineteenth century) were certainly enormous affairs in which a modern horseman would feel very far away from his horse, and undoubtedly the advent of polo was instrumental in cutting away the bottom of the full panel to make a short one (sometimes known as Rugby panel or even Whippy panel, after the firm who used it so frequently). In this it was possible for the legs to be in close contact, although there was, of course, no support in the way of a roll.

As the tree's shape was gradually altered, becoming a little deeper in the seat to comply with changing trends in equitation which involved the shifting of the rider's weight away from the rear and forward so that he was as nearly as possible over the centre of the horse's balance, so the Saumur and Continental type of panel came into being.

The Saumur, originating at the French equitation school, was narrower in the waist to allow the rider closer contact, and had an extension to the panel to afford support for the knee, and usually an additional roll placed on the outside of the panel under the flap. The whole panel was, of course, cut much farther forward.

The Continental panel is similar, but with an even narrower waist and the addition of a thigh roll at the rear. In construction it closely resembles the older type of full panel very much fined down. The thigh roll is rarely evident to the rider unless it is very heavily stuffed, and its real use is to prevent the girth straps moving back off the flap. The construction of the modern tree is such that the girth straps do occasionally tend to move to the rear, a tendency that can usually be cured by regulating the stuffing of the panel to allow the head of the saddle to fit lower (without of course touching the wither) and slightly raising the rear of the saddle.

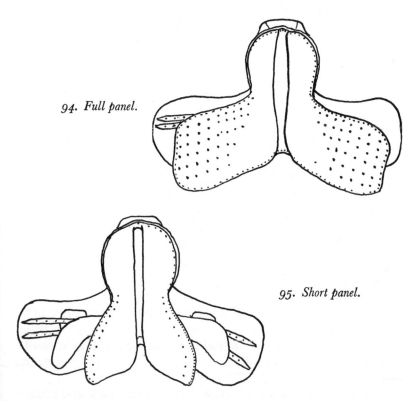

94. Full panel.

95. Short panel.

Occasionally with the modern dip-seated saddles and particularly with dressage saddles (Fig. 98), where the tree is a short one, the panel of the saddle at the rear will have an inserted gusset. This allows a greater amount of stuffing to be inserted and gives a bearing surface along the whole length of the panel. I call this gusset a Melbourne facing, or sometimes a German panel, but there are doubtless other names as well.

Of these types, the full panel and the short one are confined to the older type of hunting saddle, children's saddles, etc., while the other two will practically always be made in conjunction with a modern dipped tree usually, but not always, of the sprung variety.

96. 'Saumur' panel.

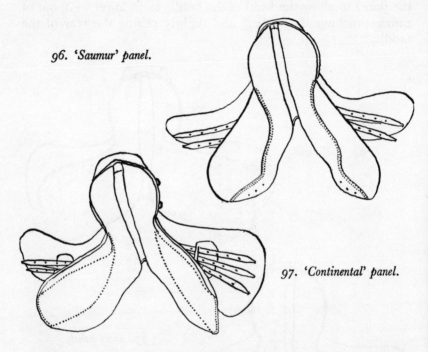

97. 'Continental' panel.

Panels can either be made of felt covered with leather or can be a 'stuffed' panel of wool with a covering of leather, serge or linen. The former is more usually found in the half panel, but it can be used and is so occasionally in a Saumur or even Continental panel.

Felt panels ensure a good close fitting to the back and require little attention, because the felt, unlike the stuffed wool panel, does not become flat and lose its resilience. If, however, an alteration to the fitting is required, the extent to which these panels can be changed is very limited.

The stuffed panel is certainly more in evidence today and by contrast does allow very considerable alteration, if required, and if properly kept has a greater resilience than its felt counterpart.

Of the materials used to cover either felt or wool panels, leather is far and away the most satisfactory. Well looked after and not allowed to become cracked and hardened with sweat, it will wear almost as long as the saddle itself, and is easy to clean and does not lose its shape. It is initially more expensive than serge, but far cheaper in the long run.

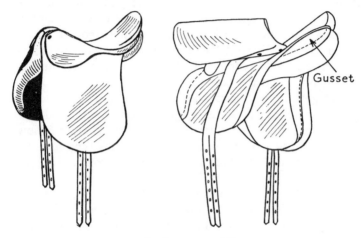

98. Dressage saddle.

Serge, a white woollen material, is not so satisfactory a covering, and is difficult to keep clean as it permits considerable absorption of sweat, which eventually penetrates into the wool stuffing, causing it to form into hard balls. The remedy is to brush the serge when it is dry and to beat the panel with a stick to prevent the wool balling. Its life is comparatively short and relining is a fairly expensive job.

Linen is harder-wearing and can be scrubbed, but should never be used on its own. It must always be put on over the top of serge, otherwise the panel wool will settle down and the linen will become loose and form creases and puckers. When it is used as an over-lining to serge, it is best to go for the unbleached variety, which is harder wearing than the white one.

With one or two exceptions, I do not believe that serge or linen are any kinder to the horse's back than well-maintained leather and certainly a dirty serge panel will cause as much trouble as anything else. One might argue that a particularly cold-backed horse would benefit from a serge lining, but I often wonder how many of these so-called 'cold-backed' horses are in reality not cold-backed but *stiff*-backed, and the reason for their cringing under the saddle is not because it is cold but because they fear the discomfort of the weight. The answer to that one I feel is to be found in the chapter (13) on Schooling Martingales.

Among those panels which were developed to prevent soreness of the back was the sorbo-rubber panel which was popular in pre-war days but now seems to have disappeared; it was introduced by Messrs Illsley of Oakham. My own objection to it would be that sorbo would both overheat and draw the back unduly and so nullify any good the panel might otherwise do.

I have used a thick plastic sponge, which does not heat the back, in a panel covered with either serge or leather and found this to be very easy on habitually tender-backed horses. There are, however, disadvantages in constructing a panel of this type and I never employed it enough to make a workable and economic proposition of it.

Another popular pre-war panel was that known as the Wykeham and very practical it was within its limitations. The panel consisted of felt so shaped and fitted that pieces could be removed or added to in order to vary the fitting. I believe they are still obtainable, but again it is a long time since I have seen one.

A new idea is an inflated rubber panel which is still in its experimental stages, but how this will work out, I am not sure, and I am not at the moment in a position to form any opinion as to its merits or otherwise.

15 | SADDLE FITTING
'Our withers are unwrung'

Saddle fitting, particularly when saddlers are not so numerous as they were, must be an essential part of the horseman's knowledge. A badly fitting saddle causes discomfort to both horse and rider and can materially affect the free movement of the horse. Ideally, the first precept to be observed is that each horse should have his own saddle. In pre-war days this was the rule rather than the exception, but today two or three horses may share the same saddle. Doubtless the economic reasons for this are sound and nothing I shall write will be likely to alter them, but, from a saddlery point of view, if not a common-sense one too, it is wrong.

Horses, like humans, may be similar in build but are never identical and the constant changing of a saddle from back to back does not give the saddle a chance to settle down to one particular shape.

I would regard my saddle both from the horse's viewpoint and my own in much the same light as I would regard my shoes. The latter are a very personal part of my apparel and have taken on the shape of *my* feet; and in the same way my saddle has moulded itself to one horse's back. I would not, therefore, want my saddle or shoes to be used by any other horse or person.

I know that this is a perfectionist outlook, but it is the correct one if the saddle is to fit the horse perfectly. Where a saddle is used on a number of horses, it may initially, if the structure of the backs is roughly similar, fit all of them reasonably well, but it will ultimately never fit one of them really correctly and it may even cause trouble in some cases. Many modern saddles are termed 'All Purpose' or 'General Purpose'. This name applies to the variety of equestrian pursuits for which the makers claim the saddle is suitable; it does not mean that it fits all animals as some would-be purchasers think. No saddle yet made will fit *every* type or shape of equine back, just as no one pair of shoes will fit all human feet.

It will always seem to me a short-sighted policy for a man to purchase a first-rate horse at the considerable price such an animal can make today, then to spend a great deal of time and more money in schooling the animal or having it schooled, and finally to risk lowering the whole standard of its performance by not buying one well-fitting saddle to use on that horse alone. A badly-fitting saddle, which causes discomfort, distracts the animal from the execution of the work in hand and can also cause a stiffness or even a hollowing of the back with the resulting constriction of movement.

Whether one accepts this advice or not, the object of fitting a saddle so that it in no way retards the horse's movement can only be attained by the observance of a few basic and common-sense principles. If these are complied with, the two main causes of soreness—pressure and friction—will be avoided. The first essential is that the tree itself must conform to the shape of the back. If it does, it can be taken that a properly made panel will follow suit and the completed saddle will fit. Trees are made in three main fittings in each of which there may be other variants; these are narrow, medium and broad. Usually a medium tree will suit the greatest number of horses, but if a narrow tree were used on a horse requiring a medium tree, the points of the tree would pinch the animal and the undue pressure would cause soreness. Conversely, a broad-fitting tree on the same animal would result in the forearch bearing down upon the withers with the same result.

Attempting to put more stuffing into the front of a saddle, whose tree is in the first place too broad, only throws the saddle out of balance and causes even more trouble. Likewise to remove stuffing from the panel of a narrow treed saddle in the hope that it will fit a broader back will be equally ineffective and pinching will still occur.

A narrow tree can be made broader by a competent saddler, but a broad tree will only revert to its original shape if an attempt is made to make it narrower.

In the conventional type of English hunting saddle, the tree has a straight head with fairly long points extending well below the stirrup bars (see Fig. 93), thus limiting the tree's capacity to fit all but a narrow range of backs within its size. The modern tree, however, where the points extend only a little under the bar, allows for a greater flexibility in fitting and when a sloped back head is also used, this too increases the number of backs which it can accommodate satisfactorily. Nevertheless, the maxim of one saddle, one horse, still holds good, and is the only real solution.

Given then that the tree fits the back, the observance of six basic principles should then make for a good fitting:

1. The saddle must afford complete clearance of the withers and also across the width and along the length of the backbone.
2. The construction of the saddle must be such that the panel bears evenly upon the back in its entirety, so that the weight of the rider is evenly distributed over as large an area as the bearing surface on either side of the backbone will allow.
3. While conforming with the above, the saddle should fit as closely to the back as possible.

At this stage I will explain these first three principles in more detail. The first one entails that the forearch or the head of the saddle must be clear of the withers, the width of three fingers between the head and the withers when the rider is in the saddle being sufficient. The channel of the panel should be deep enough and wide enough so that the weight is carried on either side of the backbone with no pressure being borne on that part at all.

In order for the channel to be of the required depth to avoid contact with the backbone, the panel must be stuffed accordingly. If the panel is allowed to become flat, the consequent pressure on the backbone will cause soreness and a restriction of the movement. A panel in this condition will most probably allow the rear of the saddle at the cantle to bear on the backbone also, with similar results.

Adequate stuffing in the panel will ensure that the channel is deep enough, but it will not affect the width of the channel which is fixed when the saddle is built. Normally the width of the channel in a well-made saddle is sufficient, but if it is too narrow or the horse has a broad backbone, pressure will occur on the sides of the vertebrae. Occasionally and more particularly with a serge panel, the two halves of the panel will close together so that the channel almost disappears and when this happens it should be rectified at once.

Personally, I like to see in a new saddle a very clearly defined channel allowing the backbone complete freedom. It is quite surprising how many sore backs are caused because of inattention to this detail and how few people appreciate its relevance.

The second principle relative to the even distribution of weight is important, and providing that the tree is properly made depends upon the even and correct stuffing of the panel.

A panel stuffed too heavily in any one place, or with one side stuffed fuller than the other, will not bear evenly on the back and instead of spreading the weight over its whole bearing surface will concentrate it in one place or another. An uneven bearing surface is not always the fault of the saddler; it can be caused by an exaggerated unevenness in the development of the horse's back accentuating the natural bend of the spine and preventing straight and balanced movement. Very often, when a horse is measured for a saddle, it will be found that the offside of the back shows greater development than the nearside. One of the objects of early training is to straighten the spine and produce even development of the muscles on each side, which is obtained by working the horse in both left-handed and right-handed circles, and so on. Where sufficient and correct training has been given, over-development of one side or the other will hardly be apparent.

Irregularities in the panel can also be caused by the rider's position. Most of us tend to ride more heavily on one side than the other, and when this is carried to the extent of riding three holes shorter on one side, as is the case with an acquaintance of mine, then the panel must be stuffed to compensate for this uneven distribution of weight. I include the third principle relating to the saddle fitting as closely as possible as a warning against panels being stuffed to such an extent that there is overmuch clearance. This is just as bad as too little as the saddle will then rock on the back, involving the second of our two primary causes of soreness—friction.

The remaining three principles are:

4. The length of the saddle must correspond to the available length of back.
5. The bearing surface of the panel must be free from irregularities and the resilience should be maintained.
6. The horse's back must be hard before being subjected to anything but short periods of pressure.

The first of these, as indeed are all of them, is a matter of common sense. A saddle that is too long in the tree—and this is rarely the case with a modern dip-seated spring-tree saddle—will put too much pressure on the loins and indeed if the rider sits on the cantle, as it is more than likely he may in the sort of conventional saddle usually concerned with this problem, irreparable damage may be done to loins and kidneys. Sore places may not appear at once, but the animal will possibly object by bucking when mounted or cringing when the saddle is put on. On the other hand, and more improbably, if a large man with a horse of corresponding size were to sit on a very tiny saddle then the weight would become concentrated over too small an area. Badly kept panels, hardened and cracked by the use of too much water, or those allowed to become lumpy or just plain dirty, will all contribute to soreness. The remedy is equally obvious.

The last of these principles is almost the most important and disregard of it is probably the cause of most sore backs. I am not a fervent admirer of the 'old days', but pre-war horsemen or possibly stud grooms did understand what it was to get horses hard. Time and again I have visited people whose horses had sore backs, sometimes red raw, to find that the animals were in what I would term soft condition and what their owners thought was 'hunting fit'. It is just not possible to bring a horse up a week before the open meet and to hunt all day without risking a sore back, if nothing worse. To expect a saddler to alter or produce a saddle to *cure* the type of back I have described is just ludicrous. The cure lies in resting the back and the prevention in plenty of slow work to harden up the muscles.

Sore backs can be caused by non-compliance with any of the foregoing, but there are other factors which will equally contribute to this complaint. The use or abuse of stable rollers, for example, is a frequent cause, for many people who would otherwise scrupulously observe my list of principles will, notwithstanding, put on a stable roller with the pads so flat that there is bound to be pressure on the spine and constant pressure at that. If a roller is used it must be stuffed and fitted with the same care as a saddle panel, and a sack put underneath flat pads is not a remedy.

It is just as essential for the backbone to be free from pressure when the saddle is on as when it is not. For this reason I always prefer the arch or anti-cast roller which does ensure such freedom.

I also encourage the use of a breast girth with a roller, in the hope that it will discourage the habit of girthing up the roller tightly. With a breast girth there is little fear of the roller slipping back and no necessity for it to be unduly tight. If a rug is used with surcingles already attached to it, the front one at least should be padded on either side of the spine and a loop left over the spine itself.

A further contributory factor is in the treatment of the back itself. Far too often the back is not given a chance to cool before the saddle is pulled off and the horse put in its box or trailer. Girths should be loosened and the horse walked until he is cool before the saddle is taken off and never, never should a back be brushed with a stiff dandy brush after hunting!

NOTE

A really bad horseman, constantly shifting and rolling in the saddle, will usually cause a sore back in time and such a man should either take riding lessons or, if too far gone for this, take up golf! Fortunately such extremes are rare, but when they do occur the guilty ones are invariably the last people to see the beam in their own eye!

The aforementioned principles apply equally to the fitting of pony saddles, but with ponies additional problems arise. I am speaking now not of the blood-like show pony whose conformation may be nearer to that of a horse, but of the good old family Dobbin kept at grass and whose figure at any time of the year approximates more to that of a barrel than anything else. Like most ponies his wither is practically non-existent and even in mid-winter his backbone is difficult to find. Fortunately, like all of his breed he is exceptionally tough and a sore back is a rarity. In many cases, however, he is so broad that the problem is how to keep a saddle on his back without it, and possibly the child too, rolling under his tummy.

Another difficulty, apart from the flatness of the back, is the problem of keeping a girth in position. The place for the girth is in the sternum curve behind the elbows and corresponds to a waistline. In the horse in work this curve is fairly well accentuated, but it is rarely found in Dobbin. Girths with a strip of pimple rubber set in the centre (like that used on table-tennis bats) will help to keep the girth from shifting, but it is also possible to induce a waistline by means of a roller. If the pony is put out in a roller some sort of waistline will appear, and one may even get a little shape on either side of that non-existent wither. The principle is much the same as that involved in wearing a belt or a corset and it does help with this particular problem!

A full panel will also assist in keeping the saddle in place because it affords greater purchase round the barrel, whereas a short panel will invariably slip. Although I am averse to a serge lining, in Dobbin's case, it does give a better grip than leather, and this property can be increased by the addition of the previously mentioned pimple rubber laid in strips along the bearing surface of the panel.

An additional girth strap known as a 'point strap' and fixed underneath the point itself, which allows the girth to be fastened to this strap and to the first of the normally positioned ones, will place the girth that much farther forward and help to keep it and the saddle in place.

Where the pony is really balloon-like and the children are small, a felt pad saddle as a first saddle is probably the best. It has no tree to worry about and the felt has a pretty good grip on the pony; it is also comfortable for the child and will conform to the shape of any back.

A more difficult matter is when the saddle habitually rides forward on a pony and after only a short time has slid up on to its neck. The problem is, of course, not difficult if a crupper is used, but few people will adopt this obvious solution. A certain amount can be done by ensuring that the saddle fits as closely as it can and by adding point straps and strips of rubber to the front of the panel, but the only absolutely satisfactory remedy is to use a crupper.

The cause of the trouble does not originate in the saddle, but in a fault of conformation resulting in a cramped shoulder with under-developed shoulder muscles and no saddle will effect a cure of this condition. Proper training aimed at freeing the muscles of the back and working the joints of hip, stifle and hocks to full capacity will encourage the opening of the shoulder and the necessary development, but this is often beyond the parent's ability and in any case takes more time than the average parent can afford. If, therefore, one has a pony of this type and is unable to do anything about it, a crupper must be the only answer. After all is it so terrible for a small child to ride its pony with a crupper on?

NUMNAHS AND WITHER PADS

Numnahs and wither pads are used in conjunction with saddles, but should not be regarded as permanent preventives against the effects likely to be caused by an ill-fitting saddle.

The apparent reason for using a numnah is to give added comfort to the back and to provide a further cushion of resilience between the back and the weight of the rider. Providing that the back is hard, the saddle well fitting and the panel well kept, I do not think there is any necessity for using them and in some cases they may even become detrimental to the comfort of the back.

My reasons against the use of a numnah are that, firstly, they cause additional heating and sometimes overheating of the back, and a back constantly overheated becomes tender and is therefore more liable to become sore. Secondly, the sheepskin variety, particularly, become saturated with sweat so that the wool becomes knotted and dirty, which may well cause irritation and soreness. Thirdly, considering the rider only, the addition of a numnah will put him that much farther away from his horse when the object in the design of his saddle, if it is a modern one, is exactly the opposite.

That many people will disagree with this view is proved by the large number of riders who do use them, and I will concede that there may be certain horses who require a numnah. I do, however, think that many numnahs are bought and used for no very good reason, and that many are put under a saddle to make the latter a better fit. The remedy in the last instance is to have the saddle properly stuffed.

The most common form of numnah is the sheepskin variety. In whatever manner it is used it will become very dirty and can be difficult to clean. It should be washed, not with a detergent or in a washing machine, but with soap flakes or better still a hair shampoo in warm, but not hot, water. It should be dried pegged out if possible so that it retains its original shape, and when almost dry the knots in the wool should be combed out. To prevent the skin becoming hard the inside should be treated with a little warm glycerine oil. Sheepskin numnahs are often lined with linen or occasionally a thin panel hide to maintain their shape. The disadvantage of a linen lining is, of course, that it makes the oiling of the skin impossible. Any numnah should be cut so that it is shaped along the centre to conform with the line of the horse's back; this will entail a join at the centre which will not usually have any detrimental effect. Incidentally, it would be almost impossible to cut a sheepskin numnah out of one skin because it would not be big enough and two skins are always necessary to make a numnah for the average modern saddle.

Felt numnahs are not now so popular probably because of the high price of felt. They have a use if a horse should have had a warble in his back leaving a lump, or if he should have a permanent protrusion caused by some previous injury. In these cases a hole can be cut in the felt to allow for these lumps and so prevent them from being rubbed. It is, of course, possible to make a 'chamber' in the panel of a saddle which will act in the same way.

A number of trainers put oblongs of felt under their saddles as a prevention against lads sitting on the back of their saddles and causing soreness under the cantle. It works, but it is an admission that the saddles are not properly stuffed and are not receiving regular attention.

The numnah of sorbo-rubber is not now in general use and it is better so, because this material both heats and draws the back. As a substitute, plastic foam has now made its appearance; it does not cause heating of the back and can be used either on its own or shaped and covered with linen. In this latter form it appears to be very satisfactory when a need for it arises.

While I am generally dubious as to the value of numnahs under hunting saddles or for general riding purposes, they do have a definite use under light racing saddles. Made either from a thin foam, covered linen or from very light-weight felt, they not only protect the back, but if cut low enough prevent the rubbing of the horse's sides by the upper half of the jockey's boots.

Wither pads I again regard as a purely racing prerogative. Few light-weight saddles can make much pretence of fitting the horse in the accepted sense, and the use of a wither pad tucked under the forearch is an essential for the horse's comfort.

In a hunting saddle a wither pad should not be necessary unless used as a temporary measure under a saddle that has begun to sink in the front. Immediately such a sinking becomes apparent the saddle should be sent to the saddler for his attention.

A good wither pad is made of knitted wool and it should be knitted right through and not just stuffed. A stuffed wither pad is pointless as the wool will work down on either side of the wither, leaving the essential part unprotected, when it is in position under the saddle.

To summarise this chapter on saddle fitting, I would say from experience that in the majority of cases where sore backs appear the fault is not in the saddle itself, but is due to bad management of either saddle or horse or both by the owner.

The majority of sore backs are caused in the early part of the season because the animal is soft and they may not become apparent until later on. Finally, once a back is sore, alteration to the fitting of the saddle panel will not cure it, although it may prevent its recurrence; the cure can be made only by common-sense treatment of the wound and by resting the back.

Before I leave the subject of saddle fitting, I must mention the question of measuring a back. It may not always be possible for you to have a saddler to your home to measure a horse or for you to take the horse to the saddler, and where this is the case a simple method of measurement can be used. It requires a piece of soft lead about 18 in. long; a piece of stout electric cable is best, which is shaped first over the animal's withers at a point approximate to where the head of the saddle would lie, and pressed well down to the shape of the back. The resultant shape obtained can then be traced on a piece of paper and the respective sides marked 'near' and 'off.' A further measurement taken nine inches or so to the rear of the first measurement and a final one taken along the length of the back from the withers will combine to give a considerable amount of information. It is also, of course, helpful to send at the same time details of your own height, weight and inside leg measurement to the knee.

It is wise to appreciate that the horse changes his shape during the period he is in work and at grass, and therefore it is better not to take such a measurement when he is fat but to wait until he has acquired a more normal figure.

To conclude, I have one pet bee among the others in my bonnet which I feel I must give an airing, and that is concerned with saddling up and mounting. The object of any connection with the horse is that we should establish an *entente cordiale*. This is hardly to be encouraged by the owner or groom who advances upon the horse with a saddle over one arm and then bangs it on to the animal's back, completing the nonsense by giving the saddle a firm slap as though that would make it stick there. The way to put a saddle on is to place it quietly well forward of the wither and slide it gently back into position.

If one has put the saddle on carefully, it is equally stupid to haul yourself up by cantle and forearch and move it out of place again when mounting. If you have difficulty in mounting easily, use a mounting block or get a leg up. With a spring-tree saddle you must be very careful how you mount. Do not put your hand on the cantle, but rather over the seat and grasp the opposite side where it joins the flap. If you use the cantle you will twist the springs of the saddle, completely upsetting its balance and probably causing a sore back.

(The parts of a modern saddle are shown in Fig. 99.)

16

THE MODERN ENGLISH SADDLE AND ITS EVOLUTION

'Hang your old saddles on the wall of your home as antiques. They might serve as a substitute for etchings.' (Count Ilias Toptani)

The modern English saddle, usually made with a spring tree and readily identified by its deep seat, sloped back head, and forward supporting rolls, is not, as some people still think, restricted purely to show jumping, although it was originally designed as such, but appears in slightly less exaggerated form as a saddle which can be used for general purposes. The modern saddle illustrated (Fig. 100) is an example of this type and, though not intended specifically for show jumping, is used in this sphere as well as for cross-country events and hunting.

The evolution of these modern saddles, whether for show jumping or for more general purposes, has its roots in the crouched forward seat adopted by the American jockey Tod Sloan and the subsequent Italian system produced by Caprilli in 1906.

Sloan's forward crouch, placing the weight over the withers and freeing the motive power behind the saddle, was a revolution in the racing world of his time and in direct variance to the then accepted principle of sitting back with the weight on the loins and behind the movement of the horse.

Caprilli's teaching went, of course, even further than this, the seat of the rider becoming a part of a complete system of scientific training.

The basic principle that the weight must be forward to free the loins and positioned as nearly as possible over the horse's point of balance at all paces is generally accepted, although few horsemen either in this or other countries conform to the pure Caprilli system in its entirety, having modified it according to their own individual thoughts and needs. It remains, however, as the basis of the modern balanced seat.

As the standard of riding has risen in the post-war period, and with interest in competitive events increasing, even greater precision is called for on the part of the rider, and the necessity for a saddle designed to assist in this respect becomes essential.

I am well aware that there is a section of the British horse community who still regard this modern type of saddle as an oddity, or at best a saddle for competitive events only and out of place in the hunting field. I intend to deal with their views later

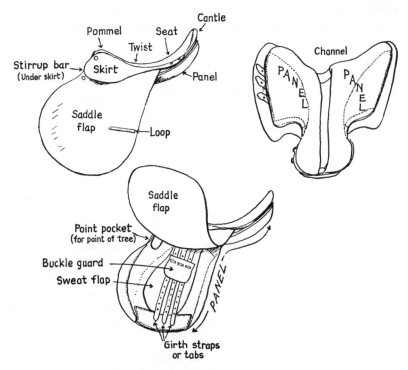

99. Parts of the modern saddle.

in this chapter, but let us first consider the object of these modern saddles—an object which must, if it is correct, and I cannot think that anyone can argue that it is not, apply basically to all forms of equitation. Very simply the object of the saddle is to provide the rider with maximum security, control and comfort, all of which are interdependent, while giving him maximum assistance in positioning his body in relation to the movement, and as near as possible to the centre of the horse's point of balance at all paces, thereby removing the possibility of the weight being carried on the loins. (It will be appreciated that the centre of balance, roughly a straight line from the withers to the ground, advances as the speed increases.)

The design of the saddle achieves this aim by:

1. A deep, resilient spring seat of such a length as to prohibit undue movement of the rider and to place him firmly in the centre of the saddle. The sprung nature of the tree, because of its resilience, allows the seat to mould itself to the rider and, in our English

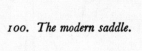 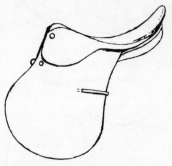

100. The modern saddle.

style of riding where seat pressure is used as an aid and as a driving agent, the force of the drive is more easily transmitted to the horse than would be possible with a tree of rigid construction.

2. A tree which is shaped to conform with the line of the back, putting the rider very close to the horse and giving him as narrow a grip as the horse itself will allow without spreading the rider's thighs.

3. Eliminating all bulk under the thighs, again preventing their spreading (*a*) by recessing the stirrup bars by placing them under instead of on top of the tree, (*b*) by reducing the width at the waist or centre of the panel, (*c*) by reducing the length of the tree points below the bar and sloping the head backwards so as to move the points forward and clear of the thigh. (*See* Spring tree, Fig. 93.)

4. The provision of a strong forward roll (*see* Fig. 99) on the panel to afford support for the thigh above the knee, used in conjunction with the sloped back head, which thus positions the bars that much farther forward than would be possible with a conventional straight-headed saddle. The positioning of the bars

and the corresponding hang of the leathers assist the rider in fixing his lower leg correctly—i.e. to the rear of the point of the knee with the toe in line and not in advance of the point. In this position the leg above the knee receives strong support from the roll, while the upper part of the leg below the knee is in contact with the horse and capable of giving immediate indications.

The overall effect then of seat, bars and roll is to anchor the lower half of the body, while allowing the rider close contact with his horse and a consequent increase in his control.

An important point to remember in a saddle of this design is the length of the girth which is used. The position of the girth straps is such that the girth buckles will lie well to the rear of the knee, and providing the length of the girth (which will depend on the individual) is neither too long nor too short, the buckles should not be felt.

The difference between a modern jumping saddle and a modern General Purpose saddle lies mainly in the shape and setting of the flap and in a slightly longer seat. In the former the flap and panel are more forward, allowing and, indeed, demanding a shorter length of leather. A jumping saddle as such is designed for one purpose and assumes that for most of the time the rider is mounted his weight will be forward over his knees, with his seat in only occasional direct contact with the saddle. While many jumping saddles are used for hunting, it is unlikely that the rider will be in a jumping position all day and occasionally a jumping saddle used for this purpose may cause trouble. The reason for this lies in the length of the leathers, which tend to put the seat a little farther back when one is sitting in the saddle and may cause the saddle to rock forward.

The more utilitarian All Purpose or General Purpose saddle allows a longer length of leather, enabling the rider to sit in the centre of the saddle, and so avoids any danger of rocking.

The conventional English hunting saddle, with a rigid tree (Fig. 101), made in great numbers between the wars and still made today was, and is, an example of very fine craftsmanship, but is so opposite in its effect upon the rider's position as to inspire Count Toptani's damning words which appear at the head of this chapter.

At its worst, its design is the antithesis of the modern saddle and of present-day thought in that its emphasis is to the rear, and its shape encourages the rider to be behind the movement and nearer to the loins if not sitting on them. If we examine it in the same way as we have examined the modern saddle, we can only arrive at these conclusions:

1. The seat is so shallow and the forearch is usually so high that the saddle tends to fall back towards the cantle. The rider's weight must, therefore, be carried more to the rear. The weight in this position, over the loins, will restrict the horse's action and may even encourage a hollowing of the back.

2. The bars are so positioned as to be under the rider's thigh and the length of the points on the straight head of the saddle also assume this position with a corresponding spreading of the thighs, often combined with an even further movement, to the rear, by the rider in order to avoid the discomfort. The lower leg in this position cannot, therefore, be in contact with the horse.

3. The tree is usually too broad in the waist by not being shaped to the back, thus spreading the thighs again. Occasionally an 'artificial' narrow grip is found which will merely increase the distance that the rider is from his horse and prevent to an even greater degree any close contact.

4. The half panel, far from putting the rider close to his horse as is claimed, is so wide at the waist that it again assists with the other factors mentioned in opening the thighs.

5. There is no forward support under the panel to assist in fixing the lower half of the body and so it becomes even more difficult for the rider to sit still and not to hamper the movement of his horse. Such a saddle cannot give security and control, or assist in the positioning of the body, to anything like the degree that a modern saddle can, however brilliant the man on top may be.

That it is possible to ride across country if not over a present-day show-jumping course in these saddles is proved by the number of people who do so. My contention is that they would ride even better and be far more comfortable if they took Count Toptani's advice and then changed to a modern saddle.

The argument that admits the worth of a modern saddle in competitive events but precludes it from the hunting-field must be fallacious. If the saddle is of value when riding in the show ring or round twenty-odd miles at Badminton, then it must be just as efficient for a day's hunting.

Recently there has been much correspondence as to whether

that gallant band of gentlemen, the National Hunt jockeys, should employ a saddle incorporating the features of a show-jumping saddle and so conform to something approaching a show-jumping seat. It seems to me that the basis of good horsemanship remains a constant factor, adaptations being made to it to suit the various branches of equestrian sport. I would have thought, however, that our jockeys had made the necessary modifications compatible to their sport with considerable success, and many of the saddles— not all, admittedly, but particularly the Australian Bosca pattern— are not far short in basic design of the principles carried out in more definite form in a modern show-jumping saddle. They have a certain dip to the seat, the rider is close to the horse, he is positioned forward and there is a certain amount of support. I have no doubt that in the future we shall see an alteration in the head of the steeplechase saddle and the positioning of the bars, where these are used, to give the saddle a closer resemblance to the show-jumping one, but I think it is unlikely that any change more radical than this will occur in the next fifty years.

As far as the seat adopted over fences goes (although in certain cases far from perfect), given a clear sight on a good jumper and allowing for the speed at which a fence is taken, the average seat, both at take-off and landing, compares well with any other. Still, if the horse is a bad jumper or is either unsighted or interfered with and finishes up by hitting a fence with his chest at 30 m.p.h., one can readily forgive any departure from the basic seat that a jockey may make. The miracle is that he stays on at all. I wouldn't claim that the average National Hunt jockey is a first-rate all-round horseman, and I doubt if he himself would, but in his chosen sport, requiring a great deal more courage than most, he is a specialist, and to criticise the occasional postures he may be forced to assume without relating them to the immediate causes is to indulge in a form of 'armchair strategy'.

If the modern saddle has a disadvantage, it is that the narrowing of the bearing surface of the panel at the waist reduces the area over which the weight is distributed. It is therefore extremely important that the panel should maintain its resilience and be carefully stuffed. Regular servicing of these saddles is essential and particular care should be taken to keep the panel clean and supple. Backs too should be hard because soft ones are the usual reason for trouble with this type of saddle.

As in all things there is good and bad, and there are saddles on the market today, not always of poor quality, whose standards of design fall below the type of saddle I have described. It is therefore wise to look carefully at any intended purchase and to discuss its features with the saddler with whom you are dealing. It is rarely satisfactory to buy a modern type of saddle in new condition at an auction sale or from any of the mushroom-type dealers who have a habit of springing up in odd parts of the country.

Particular care and attention should be given to the shape and design of the tree and the positioning of the bars.

The modern saddle has only gained popular acceptance in this country in the post-war period, although saddles designed with the same objective, even if they fell somewhat short in major aspects of design and in quality, were general in Continental countries prior to 1939. The Italian saddles made by Pariani in Milan were the best of these and are today extremely good, although I do not think the rather fragile tree they employ is suitable for the seat adopted by British horsemen. Since the inception of Toptani's jumping saddle in this country the Italian saddles have adopted certain aspects inherent in that design.

The French saddles of that period and even later are often poor in quality and are exceptionally broad in the grip. The Danloux saddle is one of the best known but employed a very weak tree and, even allowing for the difference in support (the Danloux has short thick pads, similar to an Australian buck-jumping saddle set high above the knee and a squab at the base of the flap to assist the positioning of the lower leg), was far inferior in shape and design to our own modern saddles. Often the tendency for the tree to spread so unbalances the saddle as to put the rider if anything too far forward. There were, of course, exceptions, the firm of Owen making saddles with very reasonable dipped seats.

The McTaggart saddle was another, but probably the two most significant advances were in the Santini saddle with what was then known as a 'parchment' tree and the Distas Central Position saddle. The Santini, designed by Piero Santini, did make a determined attempt to put the rider forward and had a panel which gave support. The Distas saddle was designed by Lieut.-Colonel F. E. Gibson and Lieut.-Colonel J. Hance at the time when the latter had his famous school at Malvern. This was an alliance which, but for the war, might have eventually resulted in a saddle more like the modern General Purpose English saddle of today, being produced some ten years earlier than it actually appeared. The former was originally a more than competent horseman and had been a pupil of Hance's at St John's Wood; he had travelled and had absorbed many new ideas. Almost by accident, he took up saddlery and thereafter applied himself to building a business in this line. Hance complained that he could not teach people to ride if they sat on the horse's loins, and eventually an old broken-treed Australian saddle with considerable dip in the seat was found and from this the Central Position saddle was evolved. When it was first shown at Olympia, Colonel Gibson recalls the hoots of derisive laughter it provoked, whereas today it would pass unnoticed.

Various types of jumping saddles were also produced in almost half-hearted and half-understood attempts to conform to the forward principle, most of them using an ordinary hunting tree with a forward cut flap. The shape of the head and the position of the bars combined with the flat seat to produce in the rider the rounded back with the seat in the saddle (at the back) which was taken by its exponents to be a balanced seat, and which in actual fact still placed the weight behind the movement.

After the war Colonel Gibson was again associated with another great horseman in Count Ilias Toptani. The Count was not only an exceptional horseman, but he was also intensely interested in the practical aspect of the saddle as it related to his sport. This is a rare combination and was to have far-reaching results. He had saddles made up in South America to his design and was amazed to find that neither the tree-maker nor the saddler had any knowledge of horses, and had certainly never dreamt of riding them. The same situation, of course, prevails in this country, although there are now indications of a changing attitude in this respect.

When he came to England, however, he met in Colonel Gibson a man who had much practical experience with horses as well as a considerable flair for producing improved items in saddlery. Between them they produced the Toptani jumping saddle, incorporating Toptani's ideas on the shape of the tree, its resilience and the positioning and recessing of the bars which I have described previously. The saddle was a success and was the forerunner of the various types of modern jumping saddles now available. Later,

Colonel Gibson adapted the design in conjunction with the late
Tony Collings to make a General Purpose saddle which could be
used more generally. To all these men who had the energy and
intelligence to popularise what were innovations the riding public
owes a considerable debt.

If a particular lesson is to be learnt from the foregoing, it is that
much good can ensue when the expert horseman with practical
intelligence can combine with a saddler who has enough horse
knowledge to understand his theories and appreciate his difficulties. In more recent years we have seen a further example of such
co-operation in the production of the Fulmer dressage saddle.

OTHER TYPES OF SADDLES

17

Definition of riding: 'To keep a horse between yourself and the ground'

Since the war the popularity of dressage and a clearer understanding of its aims have resulted in the appearance of a definite dressage saddle (Fig. 98).

At first, the dressage saddles produced were adaptations of the straight-flapped show saddles, and the cut-back Owen type incorporating a semi-Continental style of panel was often used. As higher standards were achieved, coupled with the influence of Mr Robert Hall's Fulmer School, which taught the classical dressage seat of the Spanish School, the shape of the saddle and its design began to resemble more closely those used at the latter establishment. Saddles made by individual firms obviously vary, but basically the design instigated by Mr Hall is followed.

The principles involved in the design of the jumping saddle, in regard to the security and comfort of the rider, remain much the same as in the dressage saddle, but modifications have to be made to conform with the different seat demanded of the rider in relation to the balance of the horse in this specialised branch of riding.

The seat is deep as in the jumping saddle, but is even shorter in length, rarely exceeding 16 in. The tree is not sloped back to allow a forward position of the bars, but is straight and the bars themselves are extended to the rear. The purpose of so positioning the bars is to allow the leather to hang down the centre of the flap, which is cut comparatively straight, permitting the rider's upper leg to lie on the flap and behind the supporting roll on the panel.

The shape of the flap and the placing of the bars enforce a very much longer length of leather, assisting the rider to sit with the upper leg above the knee just a little in advance of vertical with the lower leg drawn back, and consequently much lower than is necessary or desirable when the rider is in the shorter jumping position. In the dressage position little grip is obtained or required, but the lower leg is free and so placed as to give a finer degree of

125

control and facilitate the application of the aid either slightly in advance of the girth, on the girth or to the rear of it.

It will be appreciated that the balance of the dressage horse will move to the rear, particularly in those movements involving a high degree of collection and great lightness in the forehand, and a flap cut farther forward with a corresponding forward bar position would station the rider in direct opposition to this movement, putting him in advance of the centre of balance.

The panel employed in the dressage saddle is of the Continental type, as in the jumping saddle, allowing very close and necessary contact between rider and horse. It is important that the panel should be well stuffed at the rear, or possibly fitted with a Melbourne facing, so that the full length bears on the horse's back and so that the rider sits centrally.

Many of these saddles and all of those used by Mr Hall are fitted with two, instead of the usual three, girth straps and these are made to extend well beneath the flap of the saddle, a very short (about 30 in.) belly girth being used. The effect is to remove the bulk of the girth buckles from beneath the leg, allowing the latter to lie flat without obstruction.

It is, however, important that the girth is of the correct length, otherwise the buckles and the leather safe, fitted behind them to prevent their direct contact with the skin, will cause chafing at the elbow and will also obstruct the application of the leg when this is required to be on the girth. The use of this system of girthing is not an innovation in this country, having been used by Lord Lonsdale, and known as a Lonsdale girth, during the last century.

THE ENGLISH SHOW SADDLE

The English show saddle, confined in its use purely to the show ring, approximates more nearly to the dressage saddle than any other type, but its design is directed at displaying the horse's conformation rather than giving the rider any assistance in showing off the action of the horse. In saying this I am not implying that the show-ring horseman does not, or cannot, display the paces of his horse. I am merely stating that when he does so, he does it in spite of his saddle and not because of its assistance.

In general, the object of the saddle is to exhibit the extent of the animal's shoulder while fitting as close to the back as possible in order to display an almost uninterrupted line of the back. To achieve this the flap is cut in show saddles in a straight line from the head, or, at best, just slightly in advance of this and is occasionally even further exaggerated by being cut back to the rear of the vertical line. The seat of the saddle is normally fairly flat, and to make the saddle sit closely to the back a so-called 'skeleton' panel is used. This is always a short panel (as is the case with most show saddles) and is made of thin felt not more than $\frac{3}{4}$ in. thick, sometimes even less, covered with leather. To accentuate further the horse's front, the saddle is often placed on the back two or three inches to the rear of its normal position; and when this is done, the addition of a point strap (the extra girth strap placed under the point of the tree in order that the girth can lie farther forward) is especially necessary if the saddle is not to ride forward. A point strap is a usual fitting on almost all show saddles. As a further persuasion against the inclination of the saddle to move forward, strips of pimple rubber or corduroy can be placed on the panel to afford some grip on the back.

The straight cut of the flap necessitates the extended or set-back bars used in the dressage saddle in order that the leg may lie on the flap. Normally positioned bars on any type of tree fitted with a straight flap would result in the leg being off the flap and in advance of it.

Whether experienced judges are taken in by these little subterfuges is, I think, doubtful. After all, if they are in any doubt as to the extent of the animal's front, they are quite capable of resolving it one way or the other when the horse is stripped and run out for them. On the other hand, when the saddle is so constructed as positively to encourage the rider to sit on the cantle, forcing him to put his lower leg well forward, it seems to me somewhat contradictory to have a straight-fronted saddle to show off the animal's shoulder if one is then going to obstruct the view by sticking the leg out in front of it.

Again, I am not asserting that all show riders do sit in this position, for there are many who show in fairly deep-seated saddles, often of the Owen type and sit very beautifully. In addition, the flaps these saddles have are cut to give ample room for the knee, and there must be some advantage to be gained by giving the judge a comfortable ride and by paying him the courtesy of acknowledging that he is unlikely to be fooled as to the horse's conformation by the shape of the saddle.

127

In years to come, I think it is reasonable to expect that the dressage saddle may eventually supersede the conventional show type, and the latter's usefulness may be confined to the adornment of the walls of our homes as Count Toptani suggests.

There, too, we may find the English hunting saddle (Fig. 101) of the type illustrated. It is, however, only fair to say that many

101. English hunting saddle.

saddles of this conventional type are made today with a very much more pronounced dip to the seat than this one, and may occasionally be fitted with a modern panel of the Saumur or similar type, but even so the inherent faults in their design do not entirely disappear. The most popular type of panel used is undoubtedly the short panel either of felt or of the stuffed wool variety, the former covered with leather and the latter in either leather, serge or linen over serge. There is still a demand for this type of saddle, but, in general, there is a marked trend towards the spring-tree variety and it would seem unlikely that this will suffer any reversal.

RACING SADDLES

The making of racing saddles, especially of those weighing under 5 lb., is almost a separate section of the trade and smaller firms specialising in their production rarely venture outside their chosen field.

Racing saddles (Fig. 102) range from those primarily used for flat racing and weighing a matter of ounces and measuring perhaps 14 in. in length to the weighted saddles, as much as 30 lb. in weight, used by very light gentlemen who have to scale at 12 st. 7 lb. to ride over fences.

In the lighter saddles, made from very light pigskin throughout, stirrup bars are dispensed with, the leather being looped through a slot round the tree itself. Those over 6 lb. in weight can afford the luxury of a normal stirrup bar and also two girth straps to each side. The trees used in light-weight saddles are naturally somewhat fragile and can often be broken in one's hands, the life expectancy of saddles constructed on these trees therefore being limited.

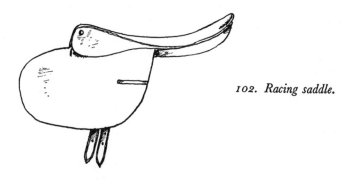

102. Racing saddle.

Panels are of the full variety, although the Australian race saddles, now enjoying a certain popularity with jockeys, have a panel resembling the Saumur type in miniature. Usually the panel is covered in cloth, silk or nylon for light-weight saddles and with serge or similar material for the heavier ones. Recently, however, an increasing number are covered in a light-weight leather, as is the case with many of the Australian ones. Leather is less absorbent than cloth, which sometimes allows sweat absorption to the point where the saddle's weight is noticeably, if one is concerned with ounces, increased by this means.

In general, the Australian trees are considerably lighter than those manufactured in this country, and while they are consequently more fragile they do allow a greater length of seat in relation to their weight than the English variety.

Few of the lighter saddles can claim to fit a horse's back in the accepted sense, and as they are invariably put on, quite correctly, as far forward as is possible, a wither pad is essential.

In order to get the saddle as light as possible, economies must be made in every direction. Apart from the size, the shape and substance of the flap, etc., the obvious place to affect a worthwhile economy is in the panel, and this is therefore reduced to the minimum; in a very light saddle the thickness of the panel between the tree and the back may not exceed $\frac{1}{4}$ in. composed of either a thin foam plastic or felt.

Light-weight saddles below 6 lb. should not, therefore, be used for anything other than the purpose for which they are intended. They are designed not for the jockey to sit in but to perch above with his seat clear of the saddle, and if used to exercise in will cause sore backs very quickly. Incidentally, it requires an extraordinarily good jockey to ride in, or to perch above, the postage-stamp area afforded to him by a light-weight saddle. The budding point-to-point rider, of above average weight, is in the initial stages best advised to use a bigger saddle and carry overweight rather than make the weight with a light saddle, and invite the possibility of taking no further interest in the proceedings after the first fence! A light-weight breast plate is also advisable with a saddle of this type, particularly over fences, and a surcingle, a 5-ft. piece of web with a buckle and leather point, is always essential in case of a slipping or even broken girth. The surcingle is put on over the top of the saddle and should lie over the girth. This position will be found easier to attain if there is either a loop on the saddle flap, or a short slit in the leather directly over the girth strap through which the surcingle can be passed.

Heavy racing saddles of 17 lb. and upwards to a maximum of 30 lb. are made to the required weight by having lead inlaid into the tree. It is important that the weighting should be put in evenly, but with more at the front than at the rear, because a saddle that has all its weight at the back becomes a further liability to the horse. My own opinion is that a weighted saddle over 22 lb. is not a satisfactory one, and it is wiser to carry the extra weight required in a weight cloth. Again when a weight cloth is necessary, the lead should be carried as much as possible in the front pockets, and the individual pieces should be shaped to fit the pockets and to interfere as little as possible with the rider's knee. The less lead one has to carry the better it is for both horse and rider, and where a not too considerable amount is required it is as well not to stint the size of the weight cloth, the weight of which can be even further increased by having it lined with a sheepskin.

RACE EXERCISE SADDLES

Trainers use for exercising purposes a larger version of the basic race saddle, known as a race exercise saddle. This is about 9 lb. when mounted with leathers, irons and girths, and although cut with a forward flap, this is not nearly so accentuated or necessary as that of the pure race saddle. Ideally, there should be a fair dip in the tree to prevent lads from riding so short that they are forced to sit on the cantle. The tree particularly and indeed the saddle itself should be as strong and as robust as possible, for if any saddle has to put up with hard wear, this one does.

In this country the panel, a full one, is always stuffed and serge-covered. Why this covering should have persisted is a problem to me, but it is rare to find any other type. Serge would seem to be the most impractical material, whether regarded from an economic standpoint or otherwise, on a saddle that gets more than its share of work and often rather less than its share of care.

A leather lining is not only easier to keep clean but rarely requires replacement, whereas serge is easily made dirty and is unlikely to last more than a season before the panel has to be relined. In addition, as I have mentioned previously, a leather panel will maintain its shape far longer. The only arguments against leather are (*a*) that it is colder to the back, and (*b*) that it would slip more easily than serge. Both these arguments do not hold water when one considers that every trainer, without exception, has an exercise sheet put under the saddle or, in the hottest weather, a stable rubber. A further argument might be that leather makes the saddle more expensive. True, it does, by a few pounds, but the additional initial cost will be more than recouped by the reduction in repair bills during the saddle's life.

For the American market, where training is carried out on rather different lines, the race exercise saddle more closely resembles its racing brother and is invariably leather lined, the panel frequently being made of felt.

At one time certain trainers used a felt-pad saddle for exercising, which instead of having a tree as we know it had just the forearch and the stirrup bars. These pads required practically no attention apart from brushing and eliminated broken trees and subsequent sore backs. They fitted almost any back and were cut well forward in the flap. For longer wear the seat and the front of the flap were often reinforced with leather. These pads are still made today and I know that George Hobbs, the show-jumping rider, uses them. I know, however, of no training stable where they are in general use.

Children's pads are made on this principle, sometimes without the additional refinement of the forearch and bars, and there is also a very useful children's leather first saddle constructed in the same way. This latter (which has a forearch) in modified form would, I should have thought, appealed to the training fraternity as a practical and certainly economical investment.

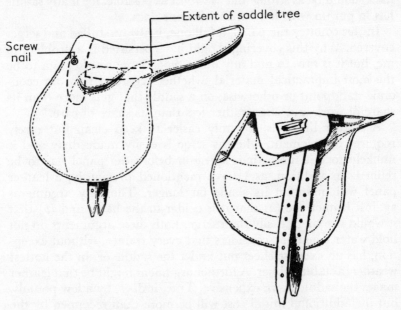

102a. Race exercise saddle, showing extent of saddle tree.

In recent months an innovation in the English racing world has been a race exercise saddle made on this principle but with the forearch having the addition of two shortened arms extending some 8 in. to the rear to give a better bearing surface on the back (Fig. 102a). The saddle is made entirely of leather with flaps and seat made in one piece and with a leather-lined felt panel. Apart from being cheaper to buy than the conventional race exercise saddle, maintenance costs are reduced to practically nil. Should the tree break the design is such that it can be easily removed by unscrewing the two nails in the head and a replacement easily fitted. An operation demanding nothing more than the ownership of a screwdriver.

Almost gone from the racing scene is the old 'short' saddle that once had a place in every training yard. It was in fact the front half of a saddle built on a forearch rather like a driving pad and about 12 in. long. The miscreant who caused a sore back by sitting on the cantle of his saddle was condemned to ride in this uncomfortable affair until the back was healed and he had had an opportunity of considering the enormity of his sins. A few still remain, but it would be rare for a new one to be asked for now.

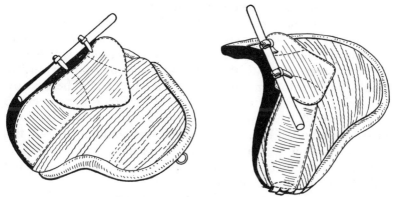

103. Felt-pad saddle fitted with 'handlebar.'

CHILDREN'S SADDLES

The purchase of children's saddles is always difficult, and although, ideally, a child's saddle should be a smaller version of a modern spring-tree saddle of the General Purpose type, few parents care to expend the comparatively large sum of money such a saddle costs until they are convinced that (*a*) the child is going to continue with its riding seriously and not regard it as another phase, or (*b*) that the child is sufficiently responsible to appreciate and to look after an expensive item of equipment.

For the very tiny on the very fat Dobbin, I think a cheap felt pad makes an excellent first saddle. The one illustrated (Fig. 103) has been fitted with detachable 'handlebars', as they are called, which consist of a stout cane covered in leather, and are easily fastened across the front of the saddle where they act first as a life-line and later as a useful means of support for the leg, particularly when the small child begins to jump. The 'handlebar' is really a simplified form of the 'Gloster' bar, which made its appearance between the wars and comprised two shaped and padded bars, which fitted over the top of the rider's thighs and had a strong spring device which gave slightly to the movement of the rider and would spring forward out of position in the event of a fall. They were termed a 'safety device' especially intended for beginners learning to jump and for those whose muscles were weak or incapacitated in some way. They have almost completely gone out of fashion, but are still occasionally obtainable and asked for by disabled persons. I cannot imagine any modern riding instructor recommending them to adult pupils of normal physique.

Following the Dobbin stage I would suggest that parents should purchase a saddle, not with a spring tree, but certainly with a good dip to the seat and with the flaps cut sufficiently far forward to enable the child to jump and ride in a modern seat. There is now an officially sponsored Pony Club saddle, which is recommended by the Pony Club as a suitable General Purpose saddle. It sells at a fixed price and, if its quality is not all that could be desired, this is not the fault of its manufacturers, but of the Pony Club officials who were responsible for fixing the price and who were no doubt activated by the best motives in so doing.

I welcome the advent of this saddle if, as I think, it will tend to encourage children to ride more correctly and to make both children and parents more 'saddle conscious', but I am sorry that it did not go further in design even if this meant a slight increase in price. This saddle does have a fairly good deep seat, but otherwise the shape of the tree, the position of the bars and the use of the conventional half panel ensure that it retains all the disadvantages of the usual hunting saddle.

It would be ungenerous to condemn a first and brave attempt at producing a general saddle at a reasonable price, but the result remains only an attempt, and there is still room for a properly designed child's saddle constructed on the same principles as the modern spring-tree type but with a cheaper rigid tree and at an economical price. Produced in the necessary quantities, such saddles should not rise in price by more than £6 or so, and there would then exist a saddle in which young people could receive the maximum assistance in riding comfortably and well. I am convinced that such a saddle will be produced within the next few years either with or without the blessing of the Pony Club. It will not, however, be produced by this body unless they first hang up their existing ideas with the rest of Count Toptani's antiques.

Lest it should be thought that I am in any way biased against the Pony Club, let me say that, as a member of my local committee and a frequent lecturer, I am not, and I have nothing but admiration for the people who devote considerable time and energy to the administration of the Pony Club. It is just that I do

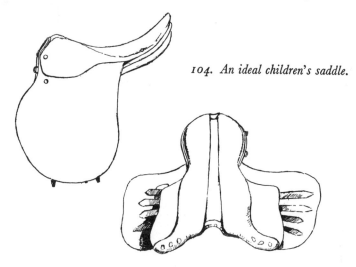

104. An ideal children's saddle.

not agree that the saddle they have sponsored is the final answer. Individual saddlers make, of course, their own versions of a child's saddle, some of them of equal merit to the official Pony Club one and at much the same price. Many make, at slightly greater cost, a very much better saddle, as the one in Fig. 104. This particular type—and it is made with very little variance by a number of firms—is almost the answer and comes very close to my own idea of an ideal child's saddle at a reasonable cost. The head of the tree and the subsequent bar position is not yet quite correct and, while an effort has been made in the waist of the panel to eliminate bulk, the tree itself is still too broad and apt to open the thighs. Nevertheless, it and others of similar construction are good robust modern saddles for the average youngster.

SADDLERY

Where possible, if only for the sake of cleaning, I would recommend a leather panel in a child's saddle.

There are a number of very cheap children's saddles on the market to tempt the unwary and possibly the uninitiated. Sale at these prices implies skimped workmanship and inferior materials and they can never be a satisfactory buy and money spent on them is in fact wasted.

18 | GIRTHS AND BREASTPLATES

'A horse is a vain thing for safety' (Psalm 33, v. 17)

Girths are usually made in 2-in. sizes from say 36 in. in length for a tiny pony up to as much as 54 in. or over for very large hunters, which measurements include the buckles.

The most expensive but undeniably the best are those made from leather, the most common varieties being the Balding, the Atherstone and the Three Fold (Figs. 105, 106, 107). The first two, though different in construction, are both shaped back from the elbow to prevent chafing in a place easily made sore if the horse is soft. The Three Fold is, as its name suggests, a piece of soft baghide folded in three. The rounded edge is, of course, in the front of the girth and this type of girth should have a piece of serge cloth or something similar laid inside the fold, so that the material can be kept greased and so feed the leather from the inside and keep it supple.

Leather girths should receive plenty of nourishment in the way of oils and greases if they are to remain soft and pliable, as their close contact with the body of the horse and the amount of sweat they consequently absorb combines with the body heat to draw

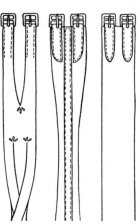

105–107. Balding, Atherstone and Three Fold girths.

out the fat content of the leather. A particularly good Balding girth can be made from red buffalo hide, and such a girth will remain supple to the end of its exceptionally long life. Web girths (Fig. 108a) are obtainable in three qualities—cotton, a union of cotton and wool, and pure wool web. The first is cheap and useless as sweat quickly rots the fabric, the second is reasonable and the third is the most satisfactory. Web girths are made and sold in pairs with one buckle at each end and are comparatively inexpensive, the wool variety having a reasonable life. They can and do, however, become hard with sweat and, if not washed regularly, will in this condition cause chafing.

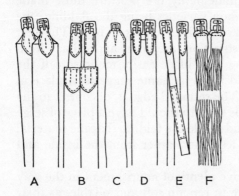

108. *Types of girth:*
  (a) *Web;*
  (b) *Web, with insert of elastic;*
  (c) *All elastic;*
  (d) *Lampwick;*
  (e) *Tubular web;*
  (f) *Nylon cord*

A   B   C   D   E   F

The hunting, or exercise, girths in web are made in a $3\frac{1}{4}$-in. width, while racing girths are made as narrow as $2\frac{1}{4}$ in. and have a correspondingly smaller buckle to accommodate the width of girth strap for which they are designed.

Surcingles, always used when racing, are made from the same web as the girths they accompany and in this capacity are correctly named. They are *not rollers*, which are fitted with pads and used in the stable or in a lighter form in the paddock.

The usual colours obtainable in girth webs are navy, blue-grey, white and one or two others. It is only possible to have racing girths, etc. made up in your own colours if you are prepared to wait (at the time of writing three months), take a reasonable quantity and pay an additional surcharge for the special weaving.

For racing, web girths are often made with an insert of elastic (Fig. 108b) on each girth so that they give to the horse as he fills his lungs. If these are used a surcingle of similar design must also be employed. Any girth can, of course, be fitted with elastic and I am surprised that more people do not have elastic inset into other types of girths, particularly for show jumping and cross-country events. There is also an all-elastic girth (Fig. 108c) much in evidence in the racing world. It became very popular some three or perhaps four years ago when it was hailed by the sporting press as an American innovation although it had in fact been made and used sporadically in this country for many years (Major E. W. O'F. Wilson of King's Lynn being one of its principal adherents). It was made in this country originally and exported to America where trainers subsequently took it up. Quite some time elapsed, however, before it was finally accepted over here. Fairly hard wearing, in spite of a tendency to rot with sweat, it does afford a good grip and certainly enables the horse to expand himself when making an all-out effort, but it needs putting on carefully and is not recommended for everyday use.

An ideal summer girth in a 3¼-in. width is one made of Lampwick (Fig. 108d), which is a tubular fabric of considerable strength and very soft indeed. It is not an expensive girth and deserves to be better known.

The show girth (Fig. 108e) in tubular web is for use with pony show saddles. It consists of two pieces of web overlapped in the centre, the join being covered with pimple rubber. This arrangement gives the girth considerable purchase on the pony and the rubber assists in keeping it in place.

One of the cheapest forms of girth is the nylon cord one (Fig. 108f) and in general it is satisfactory and will not chafe a soft horse. Unfortunately, the fixing of the strands necessitates a large and rather clumsy buckle, which is not of the best quality. A good girth deserves an equally good buckle, and I prefer an Eglantine one where the tongue lies in a groove on the top bar of the buckle. Girth buckles fitted with a roller on the top bar, as is the case with those usually used on a nylon girth, are rarely much good as the roller after a little use tends to open, cutting into the girth strap. Whatever the type of buckle employed, it is always wise to use a pair of 'girth safes' (Fig. 109) to protect the inside of the flap from coming into direct contact with the buckle; these are very cheap, whereas replacement of a flap which has had a hole worn through it is expensive. If a horse is subject to chafing by the girth, a sheepskin girth sleeve, through which the girth is passed, may act as a preventive. The sleeve should be long enough to extend just above the elbow.

A recent innovation in training stables is the introduction of polythene tubing cut in strips to correspond with the length of the girth. Although it does serve as a protection against chafing, it is principally aimed at preventing the spread of ringworm, which is not uncommon in large stables at certain times of the year. As a pair of girths may be used on more than one animal with the consequent risk of carrying infection, a sleeve of tubing is slipped over them and then burnt immediately after use, the material, which is sold in rolls of 1,000 feet, being cheap enough to be regarded as expendable.

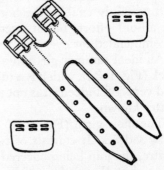

109. 'Girth safes' and girth extension.

Horses when first brought up at the end of the summer are usually fat, and in some cases girths which fitted during the season will be too short at this time of year, so that a girth extension may then be a necessary and inexpensive solution (Fig. 109).

BREASTPLATES

As far as breastplates are concerned, these are a helpful adjunct for horses whose conformation allows the saddle to slide to the rear; they are also used for racing and in parts of the country where the hilly nature of the ground makes them necessary. The straight-forward hunting type (Fig. 110), with or without adjustment on the neck straps, is the most satisfactory and is made in various weights for the particular purpose for which it is required. The ring at the breast, to which the neck straps are attached, should always, for the comfort of the horse, be backed with a leather safe. If it is necessary to have a martingale with a breastplate, either of

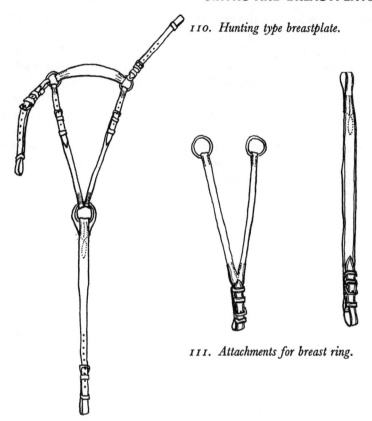

110. Hunting type breastplate.

111. Attachments for breast ring.

112. Aintree type race breastplate (web or elastic).

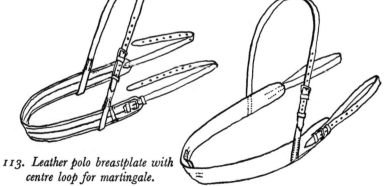

113. Leather polo breastplate with centre loop for martingale.

141

the two attachments illustrated (Fig. 111) can be attached to the breast ring. For racing a different pattern, the Aintree type (Fig. 112), is sometimes preferred and can be made either of web or elastic, the return straps in this case, however, being fastened under the flaps to the girth straps. Particular care should be exercised in the fitting of this type to ensure that the breast part is not so high as to restrict the freedom of the neck. A similar type made in leather is used for polo (Fig. 113) and here it is necessary to have a loop set on the inside in the centre of the breast part to accommodate the body of the standing martingale so as to dispense with the martingale's usual neck strap.

19 STIRRUP LEATHERS AND STIRRUP IRONS

'There is room for much to happen 'twixt the stirrup and the ground'

Stirrup leathers are made from either cowhide (usually of an 'oak bark' tannage), rawhide or buffalo hide known often as 'red leathers'. In the first two the flesh side is made to face outwards so that the grain side, which is the tougher of the two, receives the friction from the eye or slot in the iron through which the leather passes, whereas in the last case this position is reversed, the flesh side this time coming into contact with the iron. This leather is so strong, however, that there is little difference in the wearing properties of the two sides.

All leathers will stretch in use, rawhide and buffalo hide to a greater extent than cowhide. As the majority of riders place more weight in one iron than in the other, one should alternate the leathers, particularly when new, from side to side to prevent uneven stretching in any one of the pair. It is also essential to get the stretch out of a new pair of leathers before they are used for a specific event. It would, for instance, be unwise to use a new pair for the first time in a point-to-point where the rider might well find that they had stretched, in the course of his journey, to such an extent that he was forced to ride a good deal longer than he wished.

When a pair of leathers has been used for a considerable length of time, wear occurs where they pass through the iron. With red leathers this is not material, but in other types the leather should be shortened a few inches from the buckle end to allow an unworn portion to come into contact with the iron. It is helpful to have the holes on a pair of leathers numbered, and personally I like the holes punched fairly close together to enable a finer adjustment to be made. Holes so punched are termed 'half-holes' and are nearly always present in show leathers for the greater convenience of the judge.

Of the three types of leather mentioned, I would always recommend the buffalo hide because it remains supple throughout its life and is virtually unbreakable. I do in fact know of a pair still in use that are thirty years old. On account of their strength, it is unnecessary for them to be wide and thick with a correspondingly large buckle to bulge under one's thigh. For racing $\frac{5}{8}$ in. and $\frac{3}{4}$ in. are plenty wide enough, and for hunting $\frac{7}{8}$ in., 1 in. and possibly $1\frac{1}{8}$ in. for an exceptionally heavy man are the most suitable.

Light-weight racing saddles are frequently mounted with stirrup webs instead of leathers when weight is of paramount importance. The points of these webs where the holes are punched are reinforced with leather, but the remaining length is a plain tubular web. These are made in a $\frac{1}{2}$-in. width for flat racing and $\frac{5}{8}$ in. and $\frac{3}{4}$ in. for chasing.

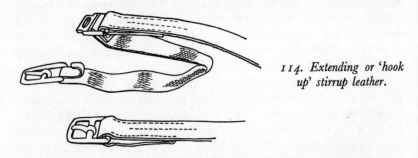

114. Extending or 'hook up' stirrup leather.

For those who find mounting difficult, or have short legs and large horses, an extending or 'hook up' stirrup leather (Fig. 114) is available. The nearside leather is fitted with a hook and slot attachment, the two parts being joined by a piece of strong tubular web. When open this allows the leather to extend downwards for some further six or eight inches, and when the rider is mounted it is a simple matter to slip the slot over the hook when the leather is again at its normal length.

Most people, I feel, would agree that a thick leather with a large buckle is a deterrent to our sitting as close as possible to the saddle and yet the majority of us persist, almost instinctively, in tucking the loose end under the existing two thicknesses of leather to form a bulge under our thigh, whereas if we just pointed the leather to the rear (after a little while it will naturally fall into this position) and passed the end through the loop which is usually fitted to the saddle for this purpose, we should have only three thicknesses and the bulge would be reduced by twenty-five per cent.

On the subject of stirrup irons, these should be made from stainless steel or one of the named mixture metals such as Eglantine. When buying them always buy an iron that is too big rather than too small and have a good heavy iron, as in the event of a fall they will free the foot more easily. If you are show jumping, or engaging in a similar sport, and are frightened of losing your iron, a piece of black mane thread connecting the iron to the spur will help you to retain it and will break quite easily should you fall.

Children's irons should be as large as possible, but not so large that the child's foot could slip right through.

There are two main variations of the basic iron which are the Bent Top iron (Fig. 120) and the Kournakoff (Fig 118). The latter was invented by the Russian cavalry officer of that name who was co-author with Captain V. S. Littauer of *Defence of the Forward Seat, Ten Talks on Horsemanship*, etc. In the former, the top is bent away from the rider's instep and, apart from encouraging him to keep his heel down, prevents the iron wearing away either the instep or the boot when boots are worn. For anyone who rides with the foot fully home this iron is particularly recommended. The Kournakoff iron goes further and is concerned with assisting and fixing the position of the foot. To do this the eye of the iron is set to one side, the inside, instead of centrally, and the sides of the iron are sloped forward with the tread sloped upwards. The result is that the foot must be carried with the toe up and the heel down and the sole higher on the outside than the inside. Such a position of the foot results in the knee and thigh being forced inwards on to the saddle. Irons of this type are usually marked as left and right and the difficulty one might experience if they were interchanged can easily be visualised. While such an iron may be of help when jumping is involved, it is not desirable so to restrict the foot position when riding dressage work.

Safety irons like the safety bars on saddles are not now so popular and as a result many of the older patterns are out of production. Wheeler's pattern, with its revolving tread and jointed sides, and the older spring tread which opened up in case of a fall are still in use, but are unlikely to be made again. The most common, the child's Peacock safety iron (Fig. 119), is still with us and undoubtedly remains the same source of exasperation for parents as it has always been. It is really an iron with three metal sides, including the tread, the remaining side consisting of a strong rubber ring stretched between a hook and a stud. The stud nearest to the tread of the iron and the rubber ring should be secured to this by a small leather loop. The open side of the iron should be on the outside of the foot, and if the child falls the rubber ring will become detached and free the foot. The trouble is that the rings

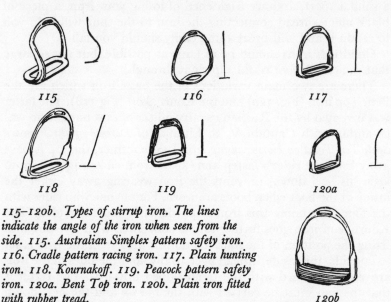

115–120b. Types of stirrup iron. The lines indicate the angle of the iron when seen from the side. 115. Australian Simplex pattern safety iron. 116. Cradle pattern racing iron. 117. Plain hunting iron. 118. Kournakoff. 119. Peacock pattern safety iron. 120a. Bent Top iron. 120b. Plain iron fitted with rubber tread.

are always getting lost or the rubber perishes and the parent in desperation has to descend to a piece of binder twine. A further disadvantage is that the tread is frequently bent downwards by the weight it takes when the child mounts. When this occurs the inside of the child's foot is higher than the outside and the knee and thigh are then opened and prevented from lying flat on the saddle.

The Australian Simplex pattern safety iron (Fig. 115) is in my view a more desirable one, although it may be a little odd in appearance. The forward bulge is on the outside of the foot and will very effectively allow the foot to be released in an emergency. These two are the only surviving members of a large family of safety irons now generally available. Possibly with the increasing prospect of meeting violent death every time we venture on to a road, we have begun to think of the horse as one of the safer means of travel and in an age of atomic brinkmanship, our instinct for self-preservation has become less strong.

Racing irons are, of course, neither large nor heavy, their weight being measured in ounces. They are usually made in a rounded shape known as a 'cradle' pattern (Fig. 116) and are either of stainless steel or aluminium.

A popular addition to the ordinary hunting iron is the Agrippin rubber tread (Fig. 120b), which slots into and over the tread of the iron to assist the rider in maintaining his foot position. The tread is particularly effective when the iron is carried on the ball of the foot or the toe, but is not of much value if the foot is pushed home unless, of course, one is using the treads with the intention of keeping one's feet warm without being much bothered about their position. If rubber treads are not used the tread of the iron should always present a rough surface to give grip to the sole of the boot.

20

BOOTS AND THE PROTECTION
OF THE LEGS

'Prevention is better than cure'

The main function of boots and bandages is, of course, to protect the legs against injuries which might occur as a result of blows, and also to give a degree of support, such support usually being associated with the tendons of the forelegs. Bandages also perform an additional benefit in the stable, or when travelling, by keeping the legs warm and are also invaluable for the treatment of swellings, etc.

The most common injuries requiring the protection of boots are those caused by brushing when the inside of the leg, usually on or in the region of the fetlock joint, is knocked by the opposite foot, or by over-reaching when the hind toes strike into the rear of the foreleg, or by speedicutting when the inside of the leg is struck high above the joint, usually just under the hock. The shins either of fore or hind legs may also be endangered as a result of striking an obstacle when jumping, and in the case of horses being schooled over fixed timber, a jumping kneecap may sometimes be necessary.

Brushing, over-reaching and even speedicutting are often caused by faulty shoeing giving rise to an incorrect action, and should either one of these become apparent a consultation with the farrier will often put the matter right.

In certain circumstances, however, the use of boots or bandages for either protection or support is a sensible precaution to take. This is particularly so in the schooling of young horses either for racing or for normal everyday riding. Youngsters are particularly prone to knock their legs about, and knocks which may appear superficial at the time have an unpleasant habit of developing into something more serious later on when the horse is put into strong work. The type of injury more usually found in young horses is that caused by occasional brushing. For horses in training (that is for racing) any of the lighter brushing boots (Figs. 121, 122, 123*a*, 123*b*) will give the necessary protection and can continue to be used when the animal is actually on the racecourse. These boots are likewise suitable for the horse being schooled within the restricted area of the *ménage*, but should the animal require greater protection, as he may do when he begins to work on smaller circles, any of the heavier polo boots (Figs. 124, 125), or possibly the school boot fastened with a bandage (Fig. 126), may

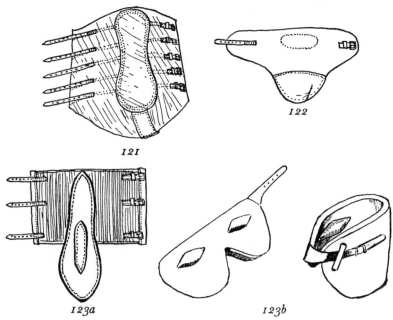

121

122

123a   *123b*

121–123b. Types of brushing boot.

be more suitable. One of the simpler forms of anti-brushing device is a rubber ring (Fig. 127) and the most simple of all is the Yorkshire boot, which consists of an oblong piece of stout rugging with a tape sewn along the centre. The boot is then doubled and tied just above the joint to form a protective cuff.

Speedicutting occurs only during fast work and either the normal type of speedicut boot (Fig. 128), made in either box-cloth or leather, or the French pattern chasing boot (Fig. 129), made usually in leather with a sorbo insert at the top, will prevent undue damage. The latter boot also prevents brushing occurring near the fetlock joint and the shins from being rapped while jumping. Another problem arising during fast work is for the point of the fetlock at the rear to come into contact with the ground, and

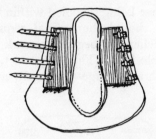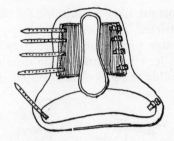

124, 125. Polo boots.

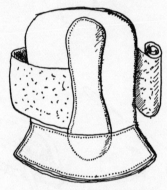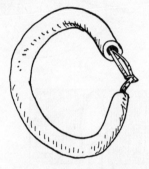

*126. School boot, fastened
with a bandage.*

*127. Rubber anti-brushing
ring.*

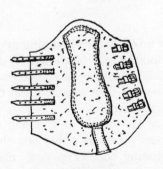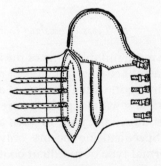

128. Speedicut boot.

*129. French pattern chasing
boot.*

although this is a difficult area to protect without restricting the
movement of the joint, a so-called heel boot (Fig. 130) is probably
the most satisfactory method of guarding against this.

A common injury sustained when jumping is caused by an over-reach and, in show jumpers, this often occurs low down on the heel or just above it. A rubber over-reach boot (Fig. 131) is usually the answer in these cases, although it may be a little awkward to get over a large hoof. Where such difficulty is experienced, the boot can be cut open and fitted with three small metal dees and

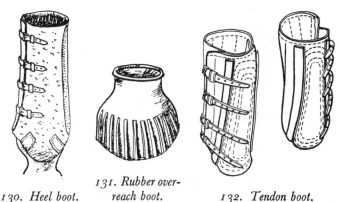

130. Heel boot.   *131. Rubber over-reach boot.*   *132. Tendon boot.*

a strap made to pass through them which will greatly facilitate the operation and make for a practical fastening. The best types of rubber over-reach boots are made from almost pure rubber, which allows considerable elasticity; they should always fit fairly tightly and should not revolve on the foot.

A more dangerous form of over-reach occurs above the joint and a strong blow here may well cause permanent damage to the tendon, if indeed it is not cut through; where there is any likelihood of such an event happening, a tendon boot (Fig. 132) should always be worn. This boot is made with a strong pad at the rear shaped to the leg, and apart from affording considerable protection also gives very strong support where any weakness of the tendon is suspected. It is usual for saddlers, when making this and similar types of tendon boots, to mark the straps 'off' and 'near' to ensure that their customers put them on correctly. While this may appear somewhat patronising, it is nevertheless often necessary, particularly as one trainer of my acquaintance used them upside down as a shin boot for the best part of twenty years!

For either show jumping, or for racing over hurdles or fences, a shin boot (Fig. 133) for both fore and hind legs will eliminate a rapped shin bone, and the French chasing boot, apart from its other advantages, is also used for this purpose.

To protect the knees of young horses when schooling over possibly fixed timber fences, the rather clumsy looking Carter-pattern knee boot should not be overlooked (Fig. 134). The strap

133. Shin boot.

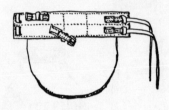

134. 'Carter'-pattern knee boot

is set on elastic and the boot is made of leather backed with ½-in. sorbo-rubber. The knee boot was perfected by Mr Len Carter of Billingshurst, and while it is undeniably not a thing of beauty it is by far the best type of knee protection. The lighter and neater

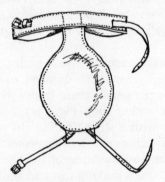

135. 'Skeleton' kneecap.

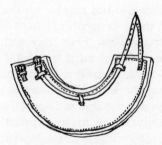

136. 'Coronet' boot.

Skeleton kneecap (Fig. 135) derived from the pattern used in the Cotswold stone wall country some years ago, and sometimes known as a 'Freeknees', also has an elastic inset top fastening and serves the same purpose, but I think it causes more restriction to the bending of the knee than the Carter pattern.

Polo ponies require the greatest protection on all four legs and their boots are heavier, being made of $\frac{1}{4}$-in. or even $\frac{1}{2}$-in. felt, and larger than any other type. Either the school boot (Fig. 126) or those shown in Fig. 124 and Fig. 125, the latter having an extension to cover the coronet, are recommended patterns. The small Coronet boot (Fig. 136) also comes within this field. Most polo boots, and often boots used for other purposes (Fig. 123), employ a width of strong elastic which, apart from giving the boot a tighter fit, is also a means of support.

Different saddlery firms will produce different patterns of boots and will market them under particular names but, in the main, they will all follow the basic design and purpose of the few types I have mentioned.

Generally speaking, boots are made from either a strong kersey cloth, which is perhaps the least practical as it gets dirty and is difficult to dry out when wet, or from the finer and lighter-weight box cloth; where a light leather is used it is usually backed with sorbo. Polo boots made of felt are, however, often reinforced with leather to give harder wear. A four-strap boot is normal for the forelegs and a five-strap one, correspondingly longer, for the hind legs.

BANDAGES

With regard to bandages, when intended to give support under working conditions, they should be of the flex variety, which give a degree of stretch without actually employing elastic; they should be put on over gamgee tissue or even over a piece of thin felt or sorbo-rubber, but for racing should always be sewn on. A recent innovation is an elasticated sock, known as Equihose and made on the same principle as the surgical stocking worn by human beings (Fig. 137). Made in three shapes as illustrated, it is suitable either for work or in the stable and has the added advantage of giving firm support while maintaining an equal tension throughout its length—an achievement rarely possible with an ordinary bandage. Its prime function in the stable is for the treatment of sprains and controlling swellings as well as for holding a dressing in place. A flex-type bandage is often applied, usually as a cold-water bandage, for similar purposes.

In racing stables it once was quite common to see a horse wearing what were known as 'cloths'. These were shaped pieces of box-cloth put on to the forelegs to support the tendon and were sewn on tightly. The horse wore his 'cloths' often in the stable as well as for work and racing, but while support was given there must have been many disadvantages in this method. There are still, however, one or two of the older stable lads who specialise in this admittedly difficult job and 'cloths' are still to be found in the training centres, but not as frequently as in past years.

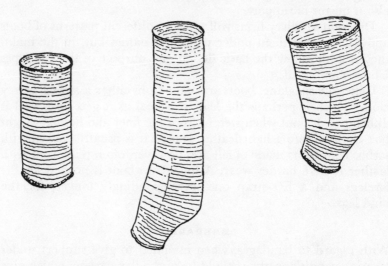

137. 'Equihose' bandages, for tendon (left), *fetlock* (centre) *and hock* (right).

Wool bandages keep the legs warm both in the stable and when travelling, a particularly good if expensive type being the Sandown bandage with a thick felted backing, which is also used for veterinary purposes.

Stockinette bandages (a tubular woven cotton) are also helpful for both work and stable, but they lack the stretching properties of the flex type for the former purpose and are not so warm as wool for the latter. They are also somewhat difficult to keep in place.

Working bandages are put on between the knee, or the hock, as the case may be and the fetlock joint, whereas a stable bandage comes lower enveloping the joint. Working bandages are either 3 in. or 4 in. wide and stable bandages 5 in., and neither should be less than 8 ft. in length excluding tapes.

As a precaution against a horse treading on himself while travelling, a wise investment is a set of the school type felt boots, while for those who tend to bump their hocks when in a horse box or stable, a pair of thick felt hock boots (Fig. 138), again with the top strap set on elastic, will act as a safeguard. Hock boots made of rugging are rarely satisfactory.

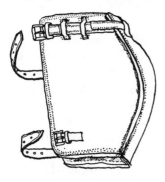
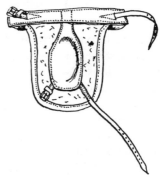

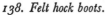

138. Felt hock boots.   *139. Travelling kneecap.*

Kneecaps (Fig. 139), sometimes of the Skeleton pattern, are occasionally used for exercising, although this quite sensible practice is now on the decline. They should, however, always be worn by a horse travelling any distance and should be carefully fitted to ensure that they do not hamper the knee movement. Boots in the hunting-field are rarely satisfactory, and if at all possible it is as well to do without them. The boot itself will very soon wear out and at the end of a day the mud it collects both inside and out can hardly contribute to any beneficial effect.

21

RUGS AND ROLLERS

'The outside is important, but the warmth comes from what you put in his belly'

The most important item of clothing and the one which receives the hardest wear is the night or stable rug. It is made either from jute of various qualities or from a finely woven canvas and is fully lined with blanketing, although cheaper types made from a lightweight jute may be only half lined. A heavy jute or canvas rug fully lined, however, will give good wear, will stand up to washing, and will not tear as easily as the lighter and cheaper qualities. The cheap variety, cut as an oblong ending at the shoulder and fastened round the chest with a hemp breast girth, are bought by many of the bloodstock agencies for shipping purposes, but are not satisfactory in a normal stable.

I have previously mentioned the importance of fitting and securing the night rug so as to avoid damaging the back, and in my experience the attached surcingles as shown in Fig. 140 are less likely to cause trouble than any other form of fastening. Racing trainers almost invariably employ this or a similar method and one will rarely find a roller in their yards. The forward surcingle is padded on either side of the rug and a loop is made over the spine itself, thereby avoiding any constant pressure. The second surcingle can be sewn flat on to the rug and helps to keep it in place, although it is not necessary for this to be adjusted tightly. A cheap rug may be fitted with only one surcingle sewn flat, but this method neither removes pressure from the spine nor does it keep the rug in position.

Most rugs, even with the surcingles fitted in the manner described, tend to rub at the top of the neck some six inches forward of the wither. A piece of sheepskin tacked to the inside of the neckpiece will largely obviate this, and in certain cases a piece of thick felt fitted on the inside of the rug a few inches below the wither on either side will raise the rug and avoid undue pressure.

Another satisfactory method of securing the rug is for the surcingles to be sewn at an angle on to the flanks of the rug halfway between top and bottom and to cross under the belly.

A good night rug should be fitted with eyelets at the rear to allow a fillet or tail string to be fitted. Such a tail string of braided cotton or even a leather strap will then prevent the rug from sliding forward. Where a separate roller is used in place of attached

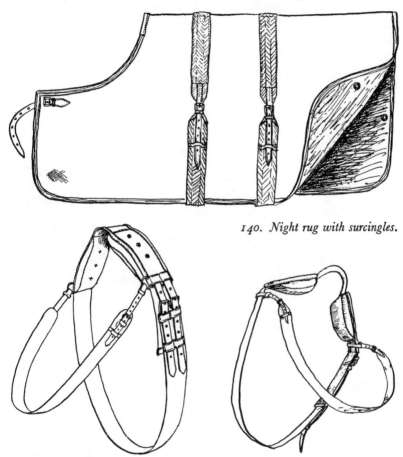

140. Night rug with surcingles.

141. Plain roller.   *142. Arch roller.*

surcingles, the pads should be kept well stuffed to avoid pressure on the spine, and a breast girth should always be employed so that there is no necessity to girth the roller up too tightly. Apart from the plain roller (Fig. 141), there are various patterns of arch roller (Fig. 142), known as anti-cast rollers, and they do certainly

157

answer this purpose and prevent a horse from rolling over. More important (from the fitting viewpoint) is the fact that they remove all pressure from the spine.

Not everyone, I think, appreciates that a roller should be fitted as carefully as a saddle and a fairly recent innovation is the adjustable arch roller (Fig. 143), with the pads set on hinges so that the roller will conform to the shape of any back. Rollers are normally made in either 4-in., 4½-in. or 5-in. widths and can be of jute web (cheap and very unsatisfactory), hemp web, wool web or leather.

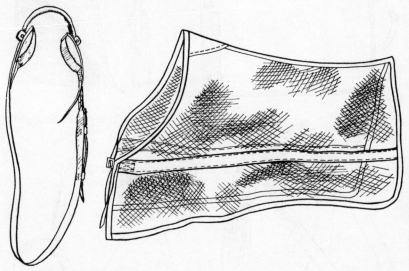

143. Adjustable arch roller.   *144. Anti-sweat rug.*

The stabled horse will also require an under blanket. Traditionally these are fawn with black, red and blue stripes on either side. A full-size blanket will weigh either 7 lb. or 8 lb. and will measure 72 in. × 81 in., while lighter-weight blankets are correspondingly smaller. Such blankets are normally sold by the 1-lb weight and are never inexpensive.

Also used in the stable as well as for travelling and in the paddock is the now familiar anti-sweat rug known in its original form as the *Aerborn* sheet (Fig. 144). The rug is made in a large cellular cotton mesh and employs the same principles as the string vest. The mesh creates air pockets next to the body, which are a form of insulation, and by so doing assists the horse to cool off without becoming chilled and also prevents his 'breaking out' in a muck sweat, with a consequent loss of condition, after hunting, racing or travelling. In the stable worn next to the skin, the rug again insulates the body against both cold and heat. It should be noted, however, that the rug should always be used with an additional top sheet; otherwise the layer of insulating air pockets cannot be formed and it becomes of little practical value. Even so it is a common enough sight at any race meeting to see horses wearing sweat rugs without any top covering. Used or misused in this way the rug may act as a sort of fly sheet, but is otherwise prevented from doing the job for which it was designed.

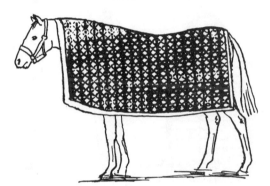

145. Cooling sheet.

The advent of the Aerborn has largely displaced the older type of cooling sheet (Fig. 145), made either from a cellular fabric or from a loosely woven wool cloth. Undoubtedly the Aerborn is one of the greatest advances in horse-clothing yet made, and credit for its introduction should be given to Colonel and Mrs Smith of Market Harborough, who were responsible for producing and testing the first rugs of this type.

For 'Sunday best', wool 'day' rugs of the same shape as the stable rug are obtainable in a variety of colours and bindings, and it is customary for these to bear the owner's initials on either side.

With regard to summer sheets, these are made from either cotton or linen, the latter being the more satisfactory, and are kept in position with either an attached surcingle or a matching roller.

A useful item of clothing when travelling is a tail guard (Fig.

146) put on over the tail bandage and made from either soft leather rugging or canvas.

Racing clothing, apart from the normal stable wear, consists of a quarter sheet, light-weight roller and breast girth and possibly a cap (Fig. 147), and when worn in the paddock is made up in the owner's colours. The everyday exercise sheets, on the other hand, are simply put under the saddle and are the same shape as a paddock sheet, but usually a few inches longer; they vary in weight according to the time of year. It is always as well to have fillet or tail string fitted on both types of sheet to prevent their being blown up in the wind.

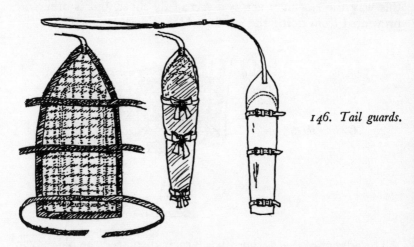

146. Tail guards.

'Gannex' cloth, too, is now beginning to appear among the exercise sheets and has certain advantages over the older wool varieties. The material itself 'breathes' as it were, eliminating excessive sweating and is also rain- and wind-proof. As it dries quickly, it is a boon for trainers with large strings, who may use the same sheets for both the first and second lots.

In cold weather, racehorses are exercised wearing wool head caps. An exercise sheet, if not put on properly, will quickly display a tendency to slide backwards from under the saddle and, dangling round a horse's hocks, may well provoke a kicking match. To prevent this happening, the front corners of the sheet should be folded up to form a triangle and made secure by lying under the girth straps next to the panel of the saddle.

In the fickle climate we enjoy in these islands a set of waterproof clothing will, on occasion, save horse and saddlery from a thorough wetting. A complete set of this is made from mackintosh fabric and consists of a rug, fastening at the breast, and a hood (Fig. 148a) as opposed to a cap, which envelops the head and the full length of the neck, overlapping the sheet as far back as the withers. The sheet is fitted with a surcingle and both sheet and hood should be ventilated to avoid sweating.

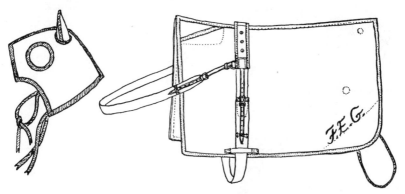

147. Paddock clothing (Cap, paddock roller and breast girth and paddock sheet).

An increasing number of horses are now kept out during the winter in New Zealand rugs, and this is an ideal way of keeping a hunter for those who could not possibly find the time to cope with a stabled horse. Generally speaking, horses kept in this way, providing they are well fed, maintain as good a standard of health and well-being as their stabled brothers and are less liable to colds and coughs. The horse can either be trace clipped, or be clipped out with the exception of his legs, but obviously, of course, there should be adequate shelter in his field or he should be brought in at nights.

Hunters normally stabled can also, in a New Zealand rug, be put out to exercise themselves when their owner is unable to exercise them.

The fitting of the rug is necessarily important and great care should be taken to avoid chafing, particularly at the top of the neck. The rug should be made of stout waterproof canvas and half lined with a thick blanketing. A fully lined rug would not be practical as the edges would soon get covered in mud.

As the rug has to keep its position whatever movements the horse may make, the method of fitting must be as secure as possible without pressure being caused on any part of the back. There are various patterns of rug, some being secured through the forelegs and some having leg straps passing between the hind legs.

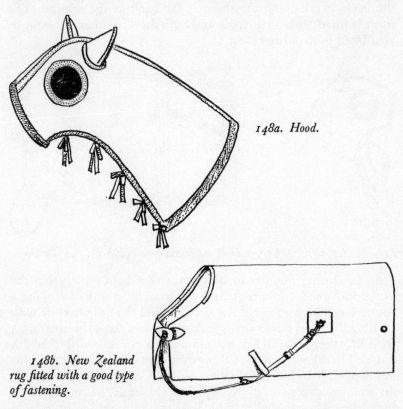

148a. Hood.

148b. New Zealand rug fitted with a good type of fastening.

Other patterns are fitted with a surcingle, but here there is a danger of chafing or causing pressure on the spine and the free passage of air along the back to dispel condensation may well be restricted.

New Zealand rugs require a certain amount of maintenance and attention if they are to give trouble-free service. Leather straps in particular should be well and regularly greased to prevent their hardening and rubbing the horse. Any fastening hooks, too, should be kept oiled and covered with a thin film of grease to avoid corrosion. A usual pattern is the one illustrated (Fig. 148*b*) and the fastening shown can, of course, be fitted to night rugs as well.

Day rugs and stable rugs, etc., are measured from the centre of the breast to the back of the rug and average measurements are as follows:

Large hunter	16·2 h.h. upwards	6 ft.
Hunter	15·2 h.h.–16·2 h.h.	5 ft. 9 in.
	15 h.h.–15·2 h.h.	5 ft. 6 in.
Pony	14·2 h.h.–15 h.h.	5 ft. 3 in.
	13·2 h.h.–14·2 h.h.	5 ft.
	13 h.h.–13·2 h.h.	4 ft. 9 in.
	12·2 h.h.–13 h.h.	4 ft. 6 in.
	12·2 h.h. and below	4 ft. 3 in. and 4 ft.

Clothing put away during the summer months should first be cleaned and then if necessary taken to be repaired before being stored in moth balls. No saddler likes rug repairs, which are rarely an economic proposition, and if he is good enough to undertake them it is only reasonable for him to expect the rugs to be fairly clean. If rugs are washed, care should be taken to see that the leather parts are not soaked in water or they should be removed and replaced when the rug is dry.

22 | STABLE EQUIPMENT AND SOME STABLE VICES

'Sufficient unto the day ...

In this chapter, which is somewhat of a miscellany, I do not intend to enumerate all the various objects which may be found in the stable and tack room, but only to discuss those which have some particular interest.

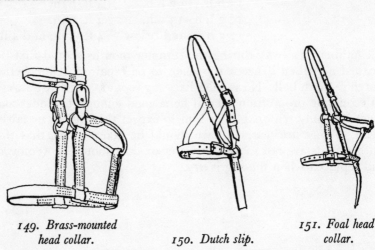

149. Brass-mounted head collar.

150. Dutch slip.

151. Foal head collar.

A good stable head collar, for instance, is an essential and there is a considerable choice, the cheaper ones being mounted with galvanised or tinned buckles and the better ones with brass. The latter adds to the cost, but will always look smarter. In addition these brass-mounted head collars may have a rolled leather throat with three rows of stitching in the cheeks and back stay (Fig. 149). The stitching looks well, but this too adds to the cost without really conferring any apparent benefit. Personally, I think a good stout head collar with the usual two rows of stitching is equally efficient. For foals and even ponies the foal slip, called a Dutch slip (Fig. 150), is easily adjusted and cheaper than an ordinary foal head collar (Fig. 151), while another adjustable type (Fig.

152), well known in racing circles as a yearling head collar, can also be used for older and larger animals.

As a matter of fact, head collars today are not of such good quality as the pre-war ones unless they are specially made. Primarily the reason lies in the public's curious reluctance to pay a reasonable price for an article which has a high labour cost and in which the best material should be used. Secondly, the stitching of head collars has traditionally been the work of female out-workers and as the older ones give up they are not being replaced. Where male labour is employed for stitching, the cost is correspondingly higher and in an article where the selling price assumes undue importance in relation to other products, economies are only made at the expense of materials and workmanship.

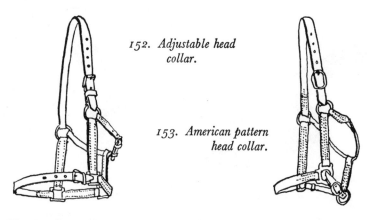

152. Adjustable head collar.

153. American pattern head collar.

Head collars made for the American market are far superior in design and quality to those produced for the home trade and there seems to be no difficulty in obtaining an economic price for them.

My own head collars follow the American pattern (Fig. 153) and are in unbreakable buffalo hide, with the head strap lined to prevent the holes stretching. They would be expensive to buy, but they will probably last for as long as I am likely to take an active interest in horses and possibly very much longer. In appearance the buffalo hide may not be so finished as a good cowhide, but it certainly is practical.

Various experiments are being made at the present time to overcome the shortage and expense of hand stitchers, and in my view the time is rapidly approaching when head collars, for stable use at any rate, will be riveted together and the public will, I think, either become accustomed to this type, which will be just as strong as the conventional stitched one, or will pay considerably more money for a hand-stitched article.

Apart from those made of buffalo hide, no head collar, even if the head strap is double lined, will stand up to a horse running back and in any case even if the leather holds, the brass rings or squares may break. If, therefore, one has an animal who habitually runs back on his head collar, it is as well to use a stout rope halter of the Yorkshire type (Fig. 154) until a cure has been

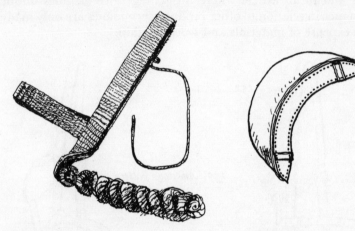

154. Yorkshire type rope halter.   *155. Felt pad for poll protection.*

effected. (A somewhat salutary method of stopping this annoying habit is to use a halter to which is attached securely an extra long lead rope. The lead rope is passed through a strong wall ring and then through the forelegs, being subsequently tied round the barrel of the horse with a slip knot. When the animal throws his head up and runs back, he merely tightens the rope round his body and the more he pulls the tighter it becomes. Obviously such a cure should be supervised and not undertaken lightly, but if the trainer inflicts one or two sharp strokes of the whip at the same time as the horse runs back, he is unlikely to have to repeat the experiment. I would, however, reserve this treatment only for hardened cases.) A halter of the Yorkshire type is always worth having in a stable and its design, incorporating as it does a throatlatch, prevents it from being pulled over the eye as is the case with the ordinary type of adjustable halter.

When a horse is travelling it may be necessary to provide him with some protection for the poll lest he should knock his head against the roof. A felt pad (Fig. 155) fitted with slots so that the head strap of a head collar can be passed through is effective, but it is necessary for the head collar to have a browband to prevent the pad sliding to the rear.

Usually a rope made with an eye or fitted with a snap hook on to the rear of the head collar is best for tying up unless one has rack chains (Fig. 156). The one illustrated has a snap hook fastening at both ends, but many trainers prefer a T- or V-shaped fastening on the grounds that the horse is less likely to damage himself on them.

Hay nets should always be used in preference to feeding hay either from the ground or from a metal corner rack. Feeding from the ground is haphazard, as far as knowing the weight of hay given is concerned, and is wasteful, while feeding from a corner rack allows the seeds to fall in the horse's eyes and in any case the rack is usually so high that the animal has to imitate a giraffe to get at his hay! A net by contrast allows the owner to weigh the amount of hay and discourages the horse from bolting his food, with a consequent benefit to his digestion. If the net is tarred, it is supposed to stop the horse chewing the cords, but I have never made up my mind as to whether it does or not, although personally I prefer a tarred net of thin cord because that seems to last longer.

It is also as well to remember that a hay net should never be hung so that when empty it hangs low enough for the horse to get a leg caught up in it. If there is any danger of this, the cord at the neck should be passed through the wall ring until the net is as high as possible, and the cord then passed through one of the loops at the base of the net before being secured to the ring. In this way the net is doubled up and there is no chance of it hanging too low when empty.

Water should always be available in the box and much as I love to see a row of painted oak buckets in a yard, that in my opinion is the best place for them. Oak buckets are heavy enough when empty and in time the inside becomes unpleasantly slimy. I much prefer the light, noiseless, rubber bucket which will suffer no ill effects if it is trodden on or even kicked round the box. If oak buckets are used they should have a metal hoop inside the rim to prevent a horse chewing at them.

Rubber is also a suitable material for muck skips, and skips so made are a vast improvement over the old heavy cane types which, with age, leave a trail of dung and straw from box to muck heap.

Grooming kits, of which the brushes are an integral part, receive hard wear and like anything else will last longer if looked after. They should be carefully cleaned with a metal curry comb after use and should be washed regularly. When drying a brush stand it on its bristles, not on its back, to allow the water to drain off. If a brush is left on its back the water will run down the bristle tufts and rot the wood into which the bristles are set.

 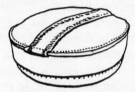

156. Rack chains.   *157. Massage pad.*

All brushes, either dandy, body, or water, are either 'machine filled' or 'hand drawn'. In the former the tufts of bristle are plugged by machine into the wood base, while in the latter each tuft is secured and wired into a base and then the wood top is screwed on. The screws and the dividing line between the base and the top are easily discernible, and although a brush of this type is initially more expensive it will give better service.

The more common Mexican whisk found in dandy brushes is now more than ever being replaced by shalon or nylon tufts in an array of dazzling colours. For those who are unable to make a hay wisp with which to strap their horses, a convenient and efficient massage pad (Fig. 157) can be made from leather stuffed with hay and is worth including in one's tool bag.

TRICKS AND VICES

Returning to horses, stabled animals have an occasional unhappy knack of developing certain tricks or vices. Many of these vices can be avoided by good stable management and by firm and sensible handling, and certainly it is always wiser to find, if you can, the cause of the trouble and put matters right from that point before embarking on one or more of the artificial methods devised to cure a specific vice. Many of the bad habits are acquired either during the early stages of training, when they are difficult to eradicate, or later on in imitation of other horses. Certain tricks are obviously inherited, while others are due to temperament. The principal vices or bad habits in the stable are biting, rug tearing, bed eating and occasionally the eating of droppings, crib biting and windsucking.

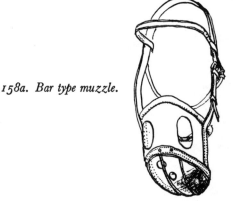

158a. Bar type muzzle.

Biting is not a very common vice, although many horses will take a playful nip when being groomed or girthed up. As far as this goes there is little to worry about providing that the play is not allowed to develop into a serious habit. If, on the other hand, you have a really vicious biter it is unlikely that mere firm treatment will have any effect. Tying him up short while grooming so that he cannot reach you is one way, or you may have to resort to a muzzle, which must be removed when not required or for feeding. The bar type muzzle (Fig. 158a) allows the animal to pick hay, etc., and is probably the most useful of its type.

Rug tearing is usually caused by boredom, although if you have a horse that is a confirmed tearer you may be forgiven for thinking it is just plain cussedness. A clothing bib of strong leather (Fig. 158b) fastened to the three squares of the head collar and bending round behind and below the chin will help in not too persistent cases, but for confirmed tearers, a bar muzzle or possibly a plain muzzle will be the answer if all else fails.

Bed eating may be caused by some deficiency in food and if this can be traced and catered for the habit may disappear. In any case the horse should have hay always in the box. Continual bed eating will effect the wind in time, but is easily cured by removing the bed and putting the horse on sawdust or peat and hoping that no other vice will develop. The depraved habit of eating droppings is similarly caused by a deficiency in the diet and is the result of bad stable management.

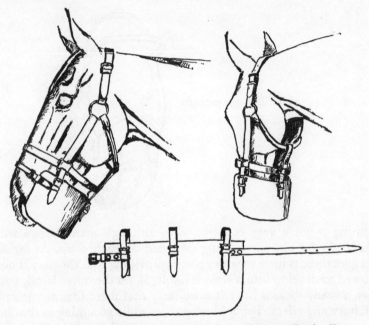

158b. Clothing bib showing method of attachment to head collar.

Two other vices, to which a horse is prone, are crib biting and wind-sucking, and they not infrequently accompany each other. The crib biter grips with his teeth any available fitting, at the same time gulping down air, while the wind-sucker swallows air without gripping a fixed object. It will be seen that by removing all fittings and protrusions from the box of a crib biter, he may then turn to wind-sucking.

A combination of both vices will cause indigestion and colic with subsequent loss of condition, and crib biting alone will result in rapid and excessive wearing of the teeth. The cause is usually idleness or boredom or it may be imitation of another horse. Removal of all fittings from the box, a liberal supply of hay to pick at and as much work and interest as possible may stop the crib biter, although it may be necessary to muzzle him except at feeding times. If, however, wind-sucking persists, then our object must be to prevent the swallowing of air and to stop him arching his neck for this purpose. A Meyers pattern cribbing device will stop it to a great extent (Fig. 159). The device is made from vulcanite

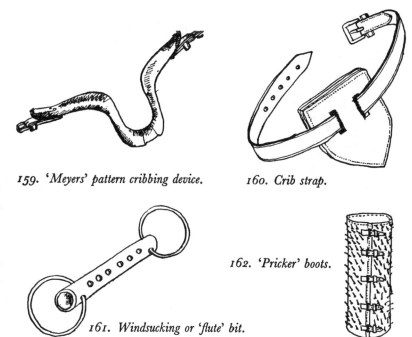

159. 'Meyers' pattern cribbing device.   *160. Crib strap.*

162. 'Pricker' boots.

161. Windsucking or 'flute' bit.

with a soft rubber centre and is strapped tightly round the gullet with a strap over the poll and fastened to the head collar to prevent it moving out of place. The simple crib strap (Fig. 160) acts in the same way, the thick leather shield shape fitting into the gullet, but is not, I think, as good as the Meyers pattern.

A wind-sucking or 'flute' bit (Fig. 161) can also be used and is probably as good as anything else. It has a perforated hollow mouthpiece which disperses the gulp of air and prevents it being sucked in.

ARTICLES FOR INJURIES

Occasionally, also, the need will arise for certain articles to cope with the treatment of injuries. A common practice is for a horse to tear at bandages on an injured leg which may be causing him discomfort; and it then becomes necessary to fit some device to

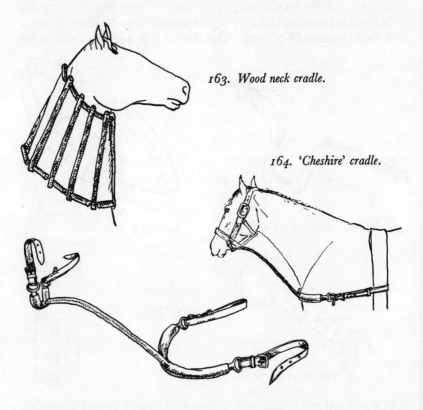

163. Wood neck cradle.

164. 'Cheshire' cradle.

prevent him doing so. The 'pricker' boots (Fig. 162), studded with tacks and put on over bandages, will undoubtedly discourage investigation, but are somewhat too barbarous to my mind and might also be a source of danger. They are frequently seen in racing stables, but I would not recommend them. At one time they were always included in the stock which my company took to our show stands at various horse events, but we eventually became so tired of convincing well-meaning persons that they

166. Walking boot.

165. Poultice boot.

167. Hinged sole boot.

168. Stuffed sausage boot.

169. Leg spray.

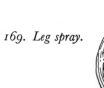

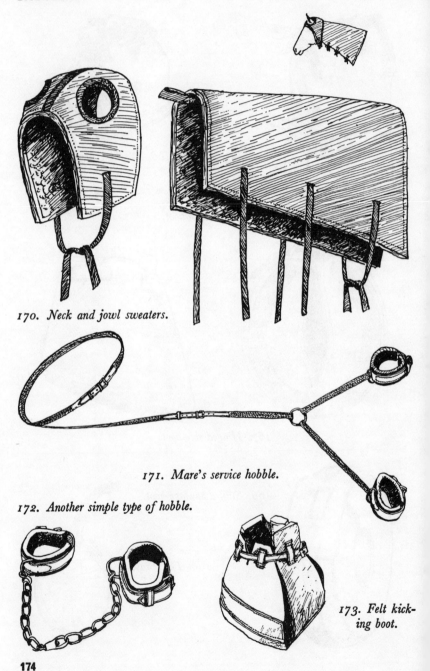

170. *Neck and jowl sweaters.*

171. *Mare's service hobble.*

172. *Another simple type of hobble.*

173. *Felt kicking boot.*

were nothing to do with making a show jumper pick his feet up, that they were tucked away in a box and only produced on request.

The wood neck cradle (Fig. 163) is more effective for keeping the head away from injuries, but it is uncomfortable and sometimes chafes. The Cheshire cradle (Fig. 164), which must be used with a roller and head collar, is a far better contrivance and is not nearly so uncomfortable.

Injury to the foot itself may necessitate the use of a poultice boot (Fig. 165) and this should be large enough to accommodate a bulky dressing. Where an injury to the foot does not require a poultice boot and when it is desirable to be able to walk the patient out quietly, either the plain walking boot (Fig. 166) or the more elaborate hinged sole boot (Fig. 167), allowing a little freedom for the frog, is a useful adjunct to a stable veterinary chest.

A capped elbow is almost always caused as a result of bruising by the heel of the shoe when the horse is lying down. When horses are liable to cap their elbows a recurrence will be avoided by strapping a stuffed sausage boot (Fig. 168) round the coronet.

A simple 'do it yourself' leg spray (Fig. 169) can be made from garden hose with a few simple fittings and can be kept in place by a sling over the neck.

One will sometimes see, more particularly in stables which concentrate on the production of ponies, the rather strange-looking articles illustrated in Fig. 170. These are neck and jowl sweaters made from a heavy felt covered with mackintosh or some similar fabric. Many ponies and a few horses are so thick through the jowl and in the neck that it becomes difficult for them to flex when required to do so. In these cases recourse is sometimes made to these sweaters to assist in the breaking down of the fatty tissues. I have personally never had any experience of these articles, but I believe they do achieve their object.

For stud work where it is necessary to prevent the mare from kicking the stallion, hobbles of various sorts are used. Fig. 171 shows the most common type fastening round the mare's neck and passing between the forelegs and attached to the hind legs. This is frequently made with a quick-release fitting in case of trouble. The simple-type hobble (Fig. 172) is also employed and occasionally a kicking strap similar to that used on cows. Many stallions are now serving mares without hobbles, but the mare wears on the hind feet a pair of thick felt kicking boots instead (Fig. 173).

23

BREAKING TACKLE

'The horse is an undisciplined force which we must strive to direct, not to extinguish'

In the breaking (or perhaps in view of the quotation above a better word would be 'making') of the young horse, our objectives are first to establish a common language between the trainer and the animal, secondly to accustom him to the imposition of discipline and authority, thirdly to prepare his physique and to give him balance by suppling and developing his muscles against the time when he will carry a saddle and rider, and lastly to *suggest* not to force, a positioning of head and neck.

The approach made by different horsemasters to achieve these objectives will naturally differ and all will have their own theories and will adapt their tackle accordingly. The articles of breaking equipment described in this chapter are therefore basic, with the possible exception of the bending tackles, Distas and Carlburg and the Barnum, and are dealt with in the order in which I would personally use them.

The first requirement in the education of the young horse will be a breaking cavesson and a lunge rein. The two cavessons illustrated (Figs. 174 and 175) are both of modern design and are very much lighter than the older type. Of the two the Orssich pattern (designed by Count Robert Orssich) is the more substantial. In this cavesson, the metal plate is hinged at the nose only on either side of the projecting ring which is mounted on a swivel, driving rings being fitted at the end of the plate on both sides. This design, placing pressure on the nose, gives great control and the swivel mounting of the nose ring facilitates the operation of the lunge rein. The Wels cavesson is very light indeed and although employing much the same principles as the other has projecting driving rings fitted to the plate itself.

The fitting of the cavesson is important and the nosepiece should be well padded to fit snugly without chafing. Personally, I would always have a throat latch fitted to a cavesson and also a brow band to prevent the cavesson shifting its position and either coming across the eye or sliding back. The fitting of a normal type of brow band may prove difficult on a youngster, and as we do not want to frighten him I would have the brow band made with its usual loop on the offside and with a slit on the nearside. A metal stud (rather like a collar stud) is fitted on to the nearside of the cavesson's head strap and the brow band is then passed across the forehead, the slit allowing it to be put on to the stud, so avoiding any chance of upsetting the animal by pulling the bridle over his ears.

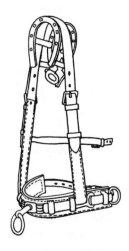

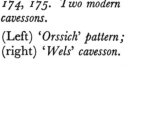

174, 175. *Two modern cavessons.*

(Left) '*Orssich*' *pattern;* (right) '*Wels*' *cavesson.*

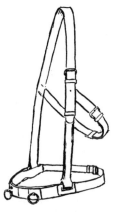

The lunge rein is made of tubular web which is light and strong and may be anything from 18 ft. to 35 ft. in length depending on individual preference. The rein is fastened to the cavesson ring by means of a buckle, and this fastening should be joined to the web by a swivel to allow the necessary movement to the rein.

The use of the lunge with the horse on a fairly large circle in the early stages (lunging on too small a circle will only restrict the action of a young horse) induces suppleness, improves the balance and teaches the horse discipline. The lunge is used throughout the horse's life to exercise him when riding is not possible and to calm him and obtain obedience.

When the time comes to introduce a bit to the mouth this can either be suspended from the cavesson by the addition of a metal dee under the cheekpiece on either side, the bit being secured by either a pair of small straps known as 'bit' straps or even by an oval-shaped spring connecting hook, or it can be fitted to a simple buckled bridle (Fig. 178).

The most common types of bit are those illustrated in Figs. 176 and 177. All are fitted with keys for the animal to play with and to 'mouth', so avoiding the danger of a dry mouth. I prefer the straight-bar bit to the jointed ones as I feel it is possible with the latter, especially if they are not fitted correctly, for the animal to get his tongue over the bit. A great many mouthing bits are too large and it is important to see that the bit is the correct size. A 5-in. bit or sometimes 4¾ in. is about right for the average hunter yearling. A jointed bit which is too big is inviting a horse to put his tongue over it.

176, 177. Two common types of mouthing bit. (Left) *Straight bar;* (right) *jointed.*

When the animal has had time to grow accustomed to the feel of the bit in his mouth and has been lunged from the cavesson with the bit suspended from it, the time will have come to prepare him for the eventual, but still distant, arrival of the saddle and later of the rider and to make the first indications as to the positioning of his head.

At this stage the trainer will require a roller (shown in Fig. 178 in two parts), a crupper and dock piece, and a pair of side reins. The roller should be made of stout hemp web adjustable on both sides for ease of fitting as illustrated, and to prevent chafing the forward edge of the roller should be shaped to the rear away from the elbow, the edge being lined with soft chamois leather. The dock piece should be made so that it is independent of the back strap and therefore more easily put on, while the dock itself is stuffed with linseed and should be kept very soft. Employment of a crupper not only keeps the roller in position, but also encourages the horse to use his loins in balancing himself.

The manner of fastening the side reins to the roller is again very much a matter of preference; many people cross the reins over the withers, as shown in the illustration, while others prefer to have them uncrossed. My own preference, for what it is worth, is to have three fastening positions on each side. The top one in the centre of the roller pad, the second some 6 in.–8 in. lower, and the third a similar distance lower again. I use the lower ones first and then move up gradually to the highest ones, which correspond roughly to the hand position when the rider is in the saddle. The

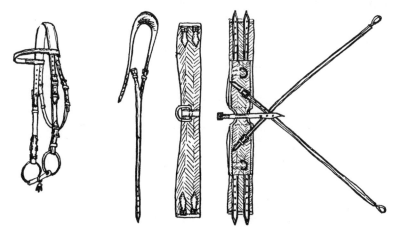

178. Simple breaking bridle, crupper and dock, roller and side-reins.

side reins I like to have inserted with elastic to avoid any dead pull and I like them to fasten to the cavesson, when the horse is being lunged, with spring hooks which are quick and easy to fit. The pressure exerted by the side reins should always be in the nature of a 'suggestion' and not a forcing of the head position desired.

It will again depend upon the trainer as to when he attaches the side reins to the bit and when he begins to use driving reins. Driving reins are similar to lunge reins, but do not require the swivel attachment necessary on the latter. Again the reins are made of light tubular web or possibly of light cord, although these will cut and burn should the horse play up and pull them through the hands.

Long reining is usually begun on the cavesson and later from the bit. The addition of large metal dee rings to the roller on either side can be made easily, if they are not there already, and the driving reins can be passed through these. When a horse persists in throwing the head up, a standing martingale attached from a central ring on the belly of the roller to the cavesson may be necessary. Some trainers still use a Cheshire martingale, in appearance not unlike a running martingale except that the branches instead of terminating with a ring are fitted with a spring hook. These hooks are snapped on to the bit rings and the effect on an unmade mouth or indeed a made one is severe.

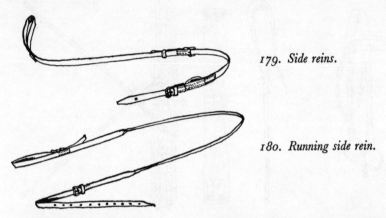

179. Side reins.

180. Running side rein.

Side reins (Fig. 179) are also effective later in the mounted training of the horse to produce a lowering of the head and are then fastened to the girth straps of the saddle. They should be used only as an occasional corrective and always be fitted with elastic. Obviously they are only an additional schooling aid in obtaining a head position and the horse could not be asked by any sensible rider to jump or to go across country while wearing them. Where side reins are used inside a school, a running side rein (Fig. 180), made in one piece with rounded leather and passing through a ring at the rear of the noseband, will permit an easier and more correct lateral movement of the head and neck while still maintaining the head position.

BENDING TACKLE

In the later stages of training bending tackle of a similar nature to the Distas type (Fig. 181) may be found by the trainer further to supple the back and to assist the engagement of hocks and loins and so produce a desirable head carriage.

I have no doubt that many of the more advanced horsemasters will disagree with the use of such a tackle and hold that with correct training methods there is no need for such articles. Possibly they are right, but nevertheless there is a call for tackle of this type and it does achieve its object fairly quickly, which may be an

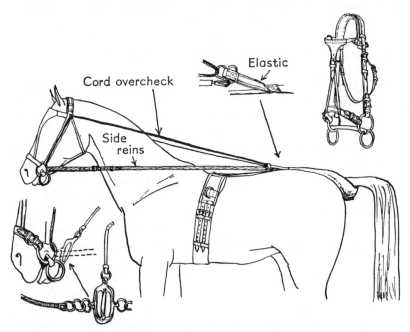

181. 'Distas' type bending tackle.

important consideration, without the restriction of the rider's weight on a young horse's back. Certainly it is well worthwhile in the schooling of children's ponies when the child is rarely strong enough in the legs to obtain a definite result and when the pony is often too small to be ridden by a stronger adult.

The tackle consists of a bridle and bit, a roller with a backstrap and dock, side reins, a Jodhphor type curb chain and cord overcheck.

The bridle is fitted with a facepiece and an elastic noseband and has a pulley on either side of the poll piece. The bit used with the bridle is known as a Wilson and has a straight bar, usually fitted with keys or rollers in the centre, and four rings. The bridle cheeks and the elastic nosepiece are both fastened to the two *inside* bit rings.

The roller is adjustable at both sides and has a large driving dee ring on the lower end of each pad as well as a ring at the belly in case a martingale is needed. The back strap has a thick piece of elastic laid on top of it just before it joins the dock, and this elastic has two rings on it—one fairly large and one smaller one. The side reins are adjustable and longer than usual to enable them to be clipped on to the larger ring mounted on the elastic of the back strap.

The Jodhphor type curb has two pieces of cord attached to the chain links on either side. This cord, when the curb is in position between the lower part of the jaw bones, is passed through and inside the inside bit rings up the head, thence through the pulley on the poll piece of the bridle. The offside cord is then passed through the smaller of the two rings on the elastic of the back strap and joins the nearside cord above the roller where they are tied together with a bow. The curb piece is prevented from falling out of position by a lip strap fastened to the throatlatch of the bridle.

To operate and fit the tackle, the roller is first put on well into the sternum curve and sloping slightly to the rear. The back strap and dock are then adjusted (equally on both sides) with a fair degree of tension sufficient to raise the tail. When the bridle has been put on and the nosepiece adjusted reasonably tightly, the side reins are clipped to the ring on the elastic at the rump. They are then carefully tightened until the head is brought into a vertical position. The pressure to achieve this position is, because of the bridle and side reins being fastened to the inside bit rings, upon the nose and not upon the mouth. The last stage is to fit the curb chain, which acts as a head raiser and will prevent the animal from becoming overbent, the necessary head position being achieved by a careful adjustment of the tension.

The tackle correctly fitted is then operating the whole horse, not just the forepart, the loins are brought into play and the horse must begin to bend at the poll and not in the lower third of the neck.

Obviously the final positioning of the horse must be approached by very gradual stages and the tackle, initially, should not be left on for more than a few minutes at a time. It is best, after first accustoming the horse to the tackle in his box, to work him quite loose in the school or in some confined space. Later he can be driven in long reins from the outside rings of the bit.

The employment of this tackle is admittedly a short cut and should not be attempted by any but the most experienced, otherwise irreparable damage might occur and resistances set up in the horse which might never be eradicated.

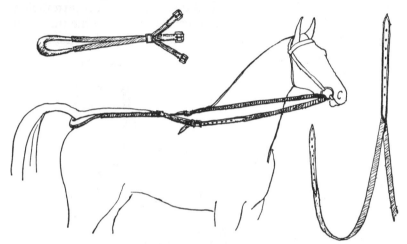

182. 'Carlburg' pattern mouthing tackle.

A very simple form of mouthing tackle is the Carlburg pattern (Fig. 182). I first made this for Captain Fergus Sutherland and, not knowing its correct name, called it Carlburg after his training establishment. The back strap ends in three pieces of elastic mounted with buckles. The side reins of web have a central strap fastened to the centre buckle, which will lie just over the wither, and then divides into two, each rein passing through the bit ring and back to the remaining buckles on the back strap. I believe it works quite well, but there is a danger of overbending the horse.

The French, in training their horses, emphasise the fact that the trainer will during the course of breaking the animal encounter the 'point of resistance'. This is doubtless appreciated by all who have to do with horses and while it may not always assume large proportions, there are horses who have a very definite will of their own and with whom it is necessary, in order to continue the training or re-training, for the trainer to assert his authority in the firmest way.

A device used by the French and by other schools of thought is the Barnum (Fig. 183). As a schooling aid for the difficult subject, it inculcates the habit of obedience and really is a simplified form of the bridle used by the American Jesse Beary, the psychology behind its application being similar. The recalcitrant pupil is brought into the school with the bridle on and, as soon as he becomes difficult, the rein is pulled tight when he will turn to face the trainer. He may continue to resist forcibly for some time, but will eventually give up suddenly and move forward to the trainer

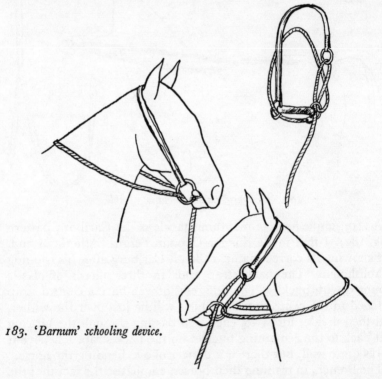

183. 'Barnum' schooling device.

who then quickly releases the now very tight cord. Benoist-Gironière in his book, *The Conquest of the Horse*, gives a full description of the Barnum and states that by this means the horse's 'obsession of the point of resistance' is broken and the habit of straining against the rein or refusing to be led is cured for ever. More importantly the horse has learnt in one sharp lesson that the trainer has the upper hand.

Benoist-Gironière in this connection quotes Gustave le Bon: 'So long as there has been no struggle the horse cannot be totally convinced of his rider's authority. Only this struggle will convince him, and it is far better that it should take place at the start rather than later on. As soon as it is over, the animal will be disciplined and once he is disciplined in one respect, he will easily be so for all the others. The battle is won, and from now on we need have recourse to nothing but kindness . . . a kindness which is quiet but never weak.'

The Barnum, whose action is clearly seen in the illustration, should be made up with a soft rubber bit and not with a metal one, which might damage the mouth. The device can also be used in place of a twitch for horses who are exceptionally difficult to clip, shoe, etc.

There are other contrivances designed to meet and break resistance in stubborn or difficult pupils when this type of treatment is necessary. Galvayne's method of throwing the animal, for instance, demands the presence of some type of hobble, but such contrivances are usually improvisations on basic breaking tackle and can be made up according to the individual's requirements.

24

SHOWING IN HAND EQUIPMENT

*'Fine dresses don't make
fine ladies—but they help!'*

Individual opinions will vary as to the most suitable tack for particular classes and the following are, therefore, only suggestions and are by no means inflexible.

A yearling, for example, can be shown in hand in a yearling type head collar with brass fittings and the addition of a white

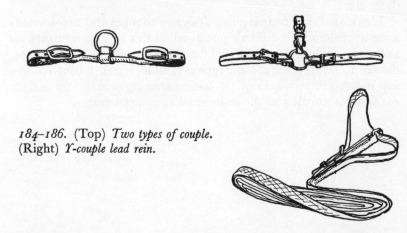

184–186. (Top) *Two types of couple.*
(Right) *Y-couple lead rein.*

buff leather brow band, a bit of the straight-bar type with keys can be suspended from the head collar squares by means of two neat straps fastened with brass buckles, and a white paddock lead rein, again with a brass buckle and about 8 ft. long, can then be fastened on to the offside bit ring and passed through the nearside ring into the hand; or, alternatively, a couple of one type or another can be employed. A common type is that shown in Fig. 184 and a better one in Fig. 185. This latter is called a 'three-way' couple, the centre strap fastening on to the rear ring of the head collar. The lead rein on the central brass ring will then be able to pull more upon the poll than the mouth, a part of the horse quite sensitive enough to give adequate control. To embrace both

187. *'Ring bit' for yearlings.*

188. *'Chifney' anti-rear bit.*

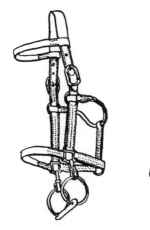

189. *'Stallion bridle'.*

190, 191. (Left) *Show head collar for stallion.* (Right) *Chain couple.*

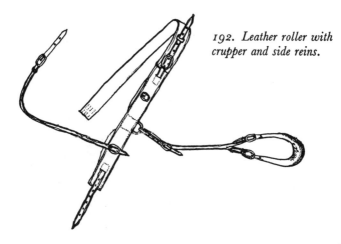

192. *Leather roller with crupper and side reins.*

187

rings of the bit and to give an even pull on each one, a Y-couple lead rein (Fig. 186) has an advantage over the usual type and is not so awkward.

A strong yearling is sometimes shown in a 'ring bit' (Fig. 187) and this type may well give increased control. The Chifney 'anti-rear' bit (Fig. 188) is occasionally used on yearlings and stallions and I can think of no better way to encourage a horse to stand on his hind legs!

Mares, if not shown in a riding bridle, can be shown in a head collar with or without a plain bar bit. There is, however, an increasing tendency for pony mares particularly to wear what used to be termed a 'stallion bridle' (Fig. 189). As it is now used on everything, I prefer to call it an 'in hand' bridle. It has neat and rather fancy brass buckles, a stitched and swelled noseband and brow band and generally shows a head off well. Ponies shown in this bridle often wear a straight-bar bit with a small and rather attractive horseshoe-shaped cheek.

Stallions usually wear a bridle of this type or possibly a stout show head collar, as shown in Fig. 190. The lead rein for a stallion will often be a leather one as long as 12 ft. and will be used with the chain couple illustrated in Fig. 191. Pony stallions (and horses, too) often have neat leather rollers with cruppers and side reins (Fig. 192), an occasional variation being to have only one side rein on the offside and a leather lead rein to the hand on the nearside.

Whips are sold by saddlers, but do not come within the scope of their trade, being made by a whip-maker whose craft it is. Every type of whip (as opposed to a stick or a cane covered with leather) has, today, either a fibreglass or a steel centre or very occasionally in the case of a race whip, it may be of rawhide. This centre is either covered with plain leather in pigskin or calf, or made by plaiting thin strips of kangaroo hide or, when not covered in leather, with plaited gut or nylon.

A few 'whalebone' lined whips may still be found, but they are not now generally produced because the supply of suitable whalebone has been stopped. The whalebone used in whip-making came from the Greenland whale, the killing of which was prohibited by International Law in 1946.

Fibreglass is a more satisfactory and expensive centre for whips than steel, allowing a lighter and better balanced article, and as used in race whips does not mark a horse as much as a steel lining, while in the long polo type of schooling whips it is firmer and less whippy than steel.

Of the coverings, plaited kangaroo hide is the most costly and probably the nicest. Gut and nylon are the cheapest. No whip is unbreakable and none will stand up to being trodden on by horses, caught in car doors or being bent double to test its resilience. If the centre of the whip is broken it cannot be repaired.

I prefer a lunge whip to be made of plain cane when the balance will be found to be very good. Steel-lined lunge whips are too heavy in the hand. Hunting whips (not hunting *crops*) are incomplete without a plaited leather thong ending in a cord or silk lash. These are the correct names for those particular items. The stock of a hunting whip ends in a flat piece of leather with a slit at the end of it through which the thong is slotted and secured. This is known as a stitched keeper. A hunt-servant's whip is a longer and heavier affair than an ordinary hunting whip, is always covered with white gut and has a white buff leather loop at the end, known as an open keeper, to which the heavy white thong is attached. Ordinary hunting whips do occasionally have open keepers, but they are not nearly so neat as the stitched type. For hunting, a hunting whip *with* a thong *and* a lash should be carried. For showing except where hunting dress is worn a plain or leather-covered cane is correct.

Spurs again are sold by saddlers and also by bootmakers, whose prerogative I suppose it is. The supply of spurs is now difficult and any out-of-the-ordinary pattern is virtually unobtainable. The most common shape is the Prince of Wales pattern (Fig. 193), with a curved neck and what are known as loop sides of uneven length, the longer one being the outside of the spur. The straight-neck pattern, however (Fig. 194), is popular for schooling as it permits more direct access to the horse. The length of the neck will vary from a very short one to one about 1½ in. long, and as a general rule the longer the rider's leg, the longer will the neck have to be to reach the horse and vice versa.

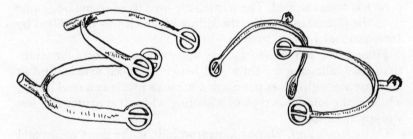

193. Prince of Wales pattern spurs.   *194. Straight neck pattern spurs.*

Spurs are either blunt or fitted with rowels which should be of the fine-point variety and need never be ultra sharp. Blunt ones are always worn to set off a hunting boot even though the counter of the boot is usually so high as to make their use impossible or at best indefinite. If a spur is worn for schooling, or even for jumping, then I think it is as well for it to be a fine-rowelled one, providing of course that the rider can control the position of his leg. A rowelled spur is a much more effective addition to the aid, and the rider is far more likely to exercise care in its application knowing that it is rowelled than if it is blunt. It is far more brutal to wear a pair of blunt spurs and to thump them into the horse's sides causing considerable bruising, as is so often seen when children and some adults appear in them.

26 CLIPPING AND GROOMING MACHINES

'How would you like to run a mile in a heavy overcoat?'

I have included this chapter in a book devoted primarily to saddlery because I feel that grooming machines will become increasingly in evidence in larger stables in the future, and because clipping machines are already a part of our stable equipment, albeit often a much abused one.

Clipping machines are among the banes of the average saddler's life, not because they are inherently faulty but because a large percentage of the people who buy them will not bother either to maintain them or to follow a few common-sense rules regarding their operation.

There are various makes of electric clipper, all of which are well made and perfectly reliable, and it is true to say that when they go wrong the fault lies in ninety-five per cent of cases with the owner or operator and not with the machine.

If a hand machine is purchased it should be first realised that the engine is small enough to be contained within the compass of one's hand and, while it is a highly efficient unit, it will only continue to function under the circumstances for which it is designed and within this capacity. Here then are a few do's and don'ts:

1. Do, for the sake of safety, operate the machine off a power point and not from a light switch.
2. Do adjust the tension screw on the blades correctly. If it is too tight, you are straining the engine and the machine will be overheated.
3. Do make sure your horse is first clean; the machine cannot cope with a thick, greasy and muddy coat without undue strain and overheating being caused to the engine.
4. Do oil the blades very frequently with a thin oil while clipping.

5. Do give the machine a chance to cool during the clipping and take the opportunity of cleaning the hair out of the blades and head.

6. Do make sure that the blades are sharp. Blunt blades will not cut and will put more strain on the engine. Blades need sharpening about twice as frequently as you think.

7. Do let the machine do the work. All you have to do is to guide it. Don't *push* it against the hair and do keep it level. By pushing the machine you are again straining the engine.

8. Do, when you have finished clipping, strip the machine and clean it and the blades thoroughly and make sure you have cleared and cleaned the air vents at the rear of the machine. Slightly grease both blades and working parts and put the machine carefully away.

9. Do read and follow the maker's instructions for maintenance.

10. Don't drop the machine on the floor and expect the manufacturer to put it right for you.

11. Don't drop the blades and expect the broken ones to be replaced.

In addition to the hand model there is also a very much more powerful hanging-type clipper with a flexible shaft to which the head is attached. This machine is recommended for use in large stables where there is a correspondingly greater demand on its services.

Electrically operated grooming machines have been made for many years, but only recently, probably because of the shortage of labour, have they been recognised as something more than a mere gadget.

The best-known make consists of two separate machines. The first is a fairly powerful motor to which is connected a flexible shaft fitted with a rotating brush capable of being revolved in either direction by a control switch. The second machine is really a glorified vacuum cleaner with a more powerful motor than the normal domestic type. It has a hose to the end of which is fixed a circular rubber-toothed pad with a hole in the centre.

This rubber head is passed over the animal with a circular motion and removes the dust, etc., from the coat through the hole in the centre of the head and into a normal vacuum cleaner bag contained in the cylinder. The massaging effect and the removal of the dirt is beneficial to the horse's well-being and the operation does not remove the natural grease. The rotating brush both cleans and puts a final polish on the coat, but care should obviously be taken to see that it does not get caught in either the mane or tail. It is possible also for the brush to be removed and to be replaced by a number of accessories such as drills, polishers, etc., as well as a clipping head.

Where possible it is preferable to reserve a box for the machines and to suspend both from the ceiling, bringing the horse to the machine instead of vice versa.

With a little practice it is possible *really* to clean a horse in about half the time normally taken when the horse is conscientiously done by hand. Stabled horses, normally fairly clean, should not require doing with the machine more than once or twice a week unless they are hunting regularly. The majority of horses—and there are numerous racing establishments using these machines regularly—very quickly get used to the machine and appear to enjoy it.

27 | THE SADDLERY TRADE
'The labourer is worthy of his hire'

In recent years the number of retail businesses specialising, largely or wholly, in the sale of saddlery has decreased and this trend is likely to continue in the future. To a great extent this is due to the acute shortage of skilled labour within the trade, a position which I think has arisen mainly because of the attitudes and economic conditions brought about as a result of increased mass production, shorter working hours and higher wages throughout industry generally. To become a craftsman requires time and application, and when conditions in the saddlery trade cannot compare with those in industry, young people are reluctant to enter it, believing it to be a dead end and on its last legs. In addition, from an executive point of view, there is the plain fact that to operate a business concerned purely with the sale of saddlery involves specific problems not always apparent elsewhere, making it one of the more difficult trades in which it is possible to earn a reasonable living in return for capital outlay and effort.

For example, to give the very high standard of service that is demanded by a saddler's customers—often under very trying circumstances—calls for specialised knowledge, heavy capital outlay in respect of stock, plus credit facilities, with consequent overheads too high for a small business in relation to the average profit mark up. As a result, many of the family businesses throughout the country, particularly where younger persons are now in control, have found it more profitable to become retailers of handbags, travel and fancy leather goods, etc., for which there is a less exacting yet ever-increasing demand, and they really remain saddlers in little more than name.

The larger wholesale firms either manufacturing leather work or saddlery hardware, and upon whom all retail saddlers must rely to a certain extent, are also confronted with similar problems and again there is an increasingly noticeable swing towards fancy goods of various types and to a decrease in the range and availability of their saddlery requisites.

As a direct result of these trends, coupled with a large increase in the riding public, a position is arising where the demand for saddlery may in time exceed the productive capacity of the trade. This is undesirable from every point of view and can only result in a lowering of standards and an increase in the already large number of saddlery 'spivs', who flit about the country picking up odd items of saddlery from the less reputable manufacturers and selling them at cut prices to those stupid enough to buy them. The 'spiv' has none of the legitimate overheads borne by the genuine trader; nor does he give any after-sales service, and the goods he sells as 'bargains' are rarely worth the low price he asks. Such trading, too, only encourages the remaining genuine saddlers to turn their attention to the easier business of leather goods retailing rather than occupying their time providing an unremunerative (to them) repair service for goods which they did not supply.

What then does the future hold for this old trade and what in fact is being done to ensure any sort of future?

Fortunately, there are two bodies able and ready to assist the individual saddler. There are the Saddlery Committee of the Leather Trades Association, whose work is concerned with every aspect and problem of the trade, and the Rural Industries Bureau, which employs not only a saddlery officer but business efficiency experts, export officers, economists and the like whose specialised knowledge is freely available for the asking.

Much, however, will depend upon the individual businessman who, however much help he receives, is ultimately the one upon whose actions will depend the future of his business. I do not think we shall see any increase in the number of retail firms purely concerned with saddlery sales, but I believe that the available business will continue, as at present, to be concentrated more and more in the hands of a comparatively few medium-sized specialist companies. The smaller one-man businesses still operating will continue to do so, but it is unlikely that they will be taken on solely as saddlery concerns when their proprietors retire.

If the specialist companies are to meet the demand satisfactorily, they will have to operate on modern lines and their first concern will have to be the building up of their labour forces, which can only be achieved by raising wages and the standard of working conditions to an attractively high level, so that a gradual recruitment of apprentices will be possible. It is indeed likely that the trade will follow the trend of 'big business', and that we shall see mergers between competing companies made with a view to cutting overheads and providing the necessary capital required to achieve this.

In addition, the number of apprentices able to be absorbed by any one firm will depend upon the number of skilled men available within the firm to carry out the training. The process of acquiring skilled labour quickly enough could, however, be assisted by the setting up of a central school with a permanent instructor financed by a group of interested companies, who would send their own young staff there for instruction. Such a scheme is not as far-fetched as it may sound, for a training centre run and backed by the Rural Industries Bureau was once operated for a short period, and this body in conjunction with the Leather Goods Association might well be able in the future to assist in the fulfilment of such a project.

If, however, production costs rise there must be either a corresponding rise in the selling price of the articles produced, or methods of production and distribution must be made more efficient and economical to absorb some part of the increased production cost. The easy way, if one is not to raise prices, is to lower the quality of materials and the standard of workmanship, but this would not only be wrong but also suicidal in a Europe united in a Common Market and in a world that still looks to Britain to produce the best in saddlery. While I believe that we can uphold this standard and that our saddlery is second to none, equally I maintain that there will always be room for improvement and that we must always be prepared to accept new ideas and institute and learn fresh techniques without disregarding altogether the old traditions.

Ultimately, I think that the price of saddlery will unavoidably have to be a little higher which, however, if kept within reasonable limits, will not affect our capacity to compete with foreign saddlery in the Common Market. German saddlery, possibly our biggest competitor on the Continent, is already considerably higher priced than our own.

The remaining increase in production costs will be absorbed by a degree of mechanisation in the making of those articles which it is not necessary to finish by hand, by the adoption of something approaching production-line techniques and by more efficient business methods.

The effect of this will be a reduction in the variety of goods made and stock held and a more rigid standardisation of design. While it will still be possible for a customer to order something to be made to his special requirements, the cost of so doing will be correspondingly high and price alone will largely eliminate orders of this kind. A firm, for instance, who may now make six different patterns of drop noseband and twenty sorts of saddle will find it necessary to reduce their range to perhaps two nosebands and twelve saddles.

Many firms are already thinking and working upon these lines and there is an encouraging tendency for saddlery companies to co-operate with each other to a far greater degree than in the past. But to my mind, the most important task facing the trade is the removal of the outdated image which has been formed in the public mind of the saddler as a little man stitching in a dark, dusty shop (a still useful relic of an era long since past), prepared to repair anything from a binder canvas to a plastic handbag at a minute's notice for practically no charge and often putting up with the insult of being knocked down as regards the price whenever he sells anything from his stock.

That this image should have arisen is the fault of the trade not of the public; and the formation of a new image of the saddler as an expert in his field and a businessman who, by providing a specialist service, is entitled, like any other specialist trader, to make a fair living (and if he has the capacity, a good one) from that section of the public who avail themselves of the service he offers, is something that must be high on the list of priorities if the trade is to attract recruits and to continue as an essential part of the horse world.

INDEX

Figures in italics refer to pages in which illustrations appear